Gene Pekarik, PhD

Psychotherapy Abbreviation: A Practical Guide

*Pre-publication
REVIEWS,
COMMENTARIES,
EVALUATIONS . . .*

"This splendid book succeeds in showing therapists, regardless of their theoretical orientation, how they can shorten their psychotherapy without sacrificing effectiveness. Pekarik emphasizes how therapists can identify a focal issue, negotiate limited but crucial treatment goals, and modify their therapeutic techniques so that they can achieve their objectives as quickly as possible–all within their own theoretical framework.

But equally important, Pekarik's book makes a forceful case for brief psychotherapy from a pragmatic, ethical, and humanitarian point of view and deals with changes that have to take place in the attitudes of therapists toward their work."

Bernard L. Bloom, PhD
*Professor Emeritus,
Department of Psychology,
University of Colorado, Boulder*

More pre-publication
REVIEWS, COMMENTARIES, EVALUATIONS . . .

"It is refreshing to read a textbook on brief therapy that is not invested in the dogma typically associated with a 'school' of psychotherapy. Dr. Pekarik offers a wonderfully successful effort to 'just state the facts' and the result is a clear and concise primer on brief psychotherapy.

In our rapidly changing behavioral healthcare industry it is important that authors, as well as clinicians, demonstrate the utility of their approach while remaining efficient and realistic about treatment goals. Dr. Pekarik's book will prove useful to any clinician wanting to remain current in their approach to treatment.

Although managed care has embraced brief therapy approaches, clinicians need to remember that the primary benefactor of efficient and effective therapy is the client/patient. Clinicians who focus on their clients'/patients' addressable needs will find greater success. Therefore, this text should not be viewed as yet another effort to provide a resource to clinicians caught in a managed care era. Dr. Pekarik's analyses and teachings were as timely ten years ago as they are now. Its just that now clinicians are more likely to listen."

James L. Johnson, PhD
Regional Clinical Director,
MCC Behavioral Care

"Gene Pekarik presents a well-reasoned, practical, and transtheoretical approach to brief treatment designed for use by therapists from virtually any persuasion. This timely effort emerges as therapists, no matter how well- or ill-prepared, are increasingly functioning in a brief-treatment environment. Recommendations are jargon-free, and concise, bullet-pointed summaries bring clarity to the complex skills required of brief therapists. Pekarik's model is research-based and the ideas presented in the book have impressive empirical support. The book should be useful to any clinician, experienced or novice, searching for conceptual and practical guideposts in the current era of diminishing treatment lengths."

Stephen F. Butler, PhD
Vice-President,
Innovative Training Systems Inc.,
Newton, Massachusetts

More pre-publication
REVIEWS, COMMENTARIES, EVALUATIONS . . .

"Gene Pekarik's new book, *Psychotherapy Abbreviation: A Practical Guide*, compellingly breaks the prevailing belief in the nexus between quality-of-care and quantity-of-service by its insistence that the road to quality is through increased effectiveness, and enhanced value. Arguing from a base of empirical research findings and meta-analytic studies and guided by a commendably balanced and practical eclecticism, this book provides a set of strategic approaches and field-tested practical hints for psychotherapists and providers to go about the complex task of acquiring focused shorter-term psychotherapeutic intervention skills in the interest of client/patient outcomes.

Psychotherapy Abbreviation offers a means to restore both the well-being of the mariners and, ultimately, the integrity of the vessel itself. And it does this by refocusing providers on what has been, for them, a stable platform: their prevailing theoretical orientation. Yet the book explicitly transcends theoretical orientation by exploiting the discrete set of common elements underlying effective care. In short, Pekarik gently guides the reader from his/her theoretical base to a full apprehension of the power of core, generic approaches—the deep common structures of effective psychotherapy upon which all helping is based.

This book is ultimately a severely practical compendium. Its power resides more in its capacity to sensitively redirect the psychotherapist/practitioner to modes of care analysis, formulation, and management. Pekarik's demystifying portrayal of these common elements, together with his analysis of the ethical and humanitarian imperatives underlying what he calls 'time sensitive approaches' to psychotherapy, are precisely the compass so many providers—and consumers—desperately need.

Finally, the uniqueness of this book lies, then, not only in its value as an instrumental means to the design and conduct of effective care, but as an indispensable values-base to advance the cause of provider accountability to the multiple sanctioners and stakeholders of psychotherapy."

Warwick G. Troy, PhD
*Director, Division of Applied Research and Professional Services;
Director, Center for Managed Behavioral Health,
California School of Professional Psychology*

NOTES FOR PROFESSIONAL LIBRARIANS AND LIBRARY USERS

This is an original book title published by The Haworth Press, Inc. Unless otherwise noted in specific chapters with attribution, materials in this book have not been previously published elsewhere in any format or language.

CONSERVATION AND PRESERVATION NOTES

All books published by The Haworth Press, Inc. and its imprints are printed on certified ph neutral, acid free book grade paper. This paper meets the minimum requirements of American National Standard for Information Sciences–Permanence of Paper for Printed Material, ANSI Z39.48-1984.

Psychotherapy Abbreviation
A Practical Guide

HAWORTH Marriage & the Family
Terry S. Trepper, PhD
Senior Editor

Christiantown, USA by Richard Stellway

Marriage and Family Therapy: A Sociocognitive Approach by Nathan Hurvitz and Roger A. Straus

Culture and Family: Problems and Therapy by Wen-Shing Tseng and Jing Hsu

Adolescents and Their Families: An Introduction to Assessment and Intervention by Mark Worden

Parents Whose Parents Were Divorced by R. Thomas Berner

The Effect of Children on Parents by Anne-Marie Ambert

Multigenerational Family Therapy by David S. Freeman

101 Interventions in Family Therapy edited by Thorana S. Nelson and Terry S. Trepper

Therapy with Treatment Resistant Families: A Consultation-Crisis Intervention Model by William George McCown, Judith Johnson, and Associates

The Death of Intimacy: Barriers to Meaningful Interpersonal Relationships by Philip M. Brown

Developing Healthy Stepfamilies: Twenty Families Tell Their Stories by Patricia Kelley

Propagations: Thirty Years of Influence from the Mental Research Institute edited by John H. Weakland and Wendel A. Ray

Structured Exercises for Promoting Family and Group Strengths: A Handbook for Group Leaders, Trainers, Educators, Counselors, and Therapists edited by Ron McManus and Glen Jennings

Psychotherapy Abbreviation: A Practical Guide by Gene Pekarik

Making Families Work and What to Do When They Don't: Thirty Guides for Imperfect Parents of Imperfect Children by Bill Borcherdt

Psychotherapy Abbreviation
A Practical Guide

Gene Pekarik, PhD

The Haworth Press
New York • London

© 1996 by The Haworth Press, Inc. All rights reserved. No part of this work may be reproduced or utilized in any form or by any means, electronic or mechanical, including photocopying, microfilm and recording, or by any information storage and retrieval system, without permission in writing from the publisher. Printed in the United States of America.

The Haworth Press, Inc., 10 Alice Street, Binghamton, NY 13904-1580

Library of Congress Cataloging-in-Publication Data

Pekarik, Gene.
   Psychotherapy abbreviation : a practical guide / Gene Pekarik.
      p.   cm.
   Includes bibliographical references and index.
   ISBN 1-56024-934-X (alk. paper)
   1. Brief psychotherapy. I. Title.
RC480.55.P45 1996
616.89′14–dc20   95-42382
                                                                                                                                 CIP

CONTENTS

Preface ix

Chapter One: Introduction 1

Historical, Theoretical, and Technical Foundations
of Brief Therapy 3
Elements Common to Most Brief Therapies 8
General Abbreviation Strategies: Introduction
to a Model 9

Chapter Two: Rationale 11

Client Expectations and Preferences Regarding
Treatment Length, Content, and Goals 11
Actual Treatment Attendance Patterns 14
Relationship of Treatment Duration to Outcome
and Satisfaction 18
Relationship of Client Characteristics to Brief
Therapy Outcome 25
Summary 25

Chapter Three: Client Selection 27

Professionals' Attitudes Toward Client Selection 27
Common Selection and Exclusion Recommendations 29
Research Findings 29
Ethics and Treatment Selection 31
Conclusions and Recommendations 33

**Chapter Four: A Model for Conceptualizing
the Treatment Abbreviation Process** 37

Contributions of "Common Characteristics"
to Treatment Abbreviation 38
The Four Key Elements of Treatment Abbreviation 42
Philosophy, Values, and Attitudes 44

Chapter Five: Rapid Assessment and Case Conceptualization — 47
Case Conceptualization — 47
Rapid Assessment — 49
Assessment Models — 51

Chapter Six: Establishing a Brief Therapy Focus — 59
Orientation to a Narrow Focus — 59
Focusing in Standard Therapy — 60
Focusing in Brief Therapy — 61
Narrowing the Focus When Multiple Problems Are Present — 65
Practice Exercise — 68
Focus Summary — 71
Integration of Assessment, Case Conceptualization, and Focusing with a Case Example — 72

Chapter Seven: Negotiating Treatment Goals — 83
Goal Selection in Standard Therapy — 84
Goal Negotiation in Brief Therapy — 85
Goal Characteristics — 86
Goal Identification and Negotiation Strategies — 87
Estimation of Treatment Durations for Different Goal Levels — 88
Case Example: Negotiating Goals and Treatment Duration — 95

Chapter Eight: Treatment Implementation: Adapting Standard Psychotherapy Techniques to a Briefer Format — 105
Integrative Model for Brief Therapy Intervention — 108
Assessment/Treatment Planning vs. Intervention: Treatment in the First Session — 113
Strategies for Adapting Traditional Techniques to a Brief Format — 115
Short-Term Goals — 116
Theory-Derived Techniques — 119
General Recommendations for Applying Interventions to a Brief Format — 121

Summary	124
Case Example: Treatment Implementation	124

Chapter Nine: Importance of the First Two Sessions — 141

Tasks to Accomplish: Session One	144
Tasks to Accomplish: Session Two	145
Tasks to Accomplish: Sessions Three through Termination	145

Chapter Ten: Issues in the Practice of Brief Therapy — 147

The Psychotherapist Subcultural Context: Resistance to Brief Therapy	148
Training and Professional Development Issues	154

Appendix A: Case Two — 159

Appendix B: Guidelines for Group Supervision of Brief Therapy Cases — 171

References — 175

Index — 187

ABOUT THE AUTHOR

Gene Pekarik, PhD, is Professor in the Department of Clinical Psychology at Antioch New England Graduate School in Keene, New Hampshire and is actively involved in all important aspects of the brief therapy field—practice, training, consulting, and research. He has published widely in the psychotherapy field, especially in the areas of treatment outcome, client satisfaction, and brief therapy.

Preface

There has been a greatly increased interest in brief therapy in recent years, primarily because of its compatibility with attempts to control treatment costs. Such pragmatic forces, bolstered by outcome research supportive of brief therapy's effectiveness, virtually guarantee that brief therapy will be the treatment delivered to most clients in the future. Many practicing psychotherapists and those currently in training have not received special training in brief therapy, however, leaving these professionals to learn the technique through postgraduate training workshops, books, and special graduate courses.

Almost all the brief therapy workshops and books are associated with a particular school of psychotherapy and its affiliated theory of human behavior. Subscription to the associated school and theoretical underpinnings is required in order to gain maximal benefit from the training resource. Some of the approaches make their affiliation explicit (e.g., Wolberg's [1980] psychodynamic approach) while others are implicit (e.g., Talmon's [1990] unnamed but clearly psychodynamic procedure). Many, such as Budman and Gurman's (1988) text, are an amalgam of theory and technique derived from complementary theories (in this specific case, focusing on "core interpersonal life issues . . . stage of life development and . . . existential concerns," p. 27).

The association of brief therapy technique with theoretical orientation in books and workshops poses major problems for many practitioners and students eager to learn how to do brief therapy. It may be quite difficult for clinicians to find a brief therapy training resource that speaks a compatible theoretical language, given the sometimes limited access to training and the often implied, unspecified, or idiosyncratic approach offered by many authors. In addition, some approaches, such as the cognitive-behavioral approach, are erroneously considered short-term by their very nature (elaboration of this issue is presented in Chapter Two) and therefore there is virtually no resource available to teach how to further abbreviate such treatment. Even when a clinician can find a training resource with a nominally compatible orientation, there can be problem conceptualization and treatment technique incompatibility because of idiosyncratic styles of the author and/or reader. Most practicing therapists have little interest in changing their basic theory or treatment techniques. Furthermore, psychotherapists appear to benefit little when exposed to training provided by someone with a different theoretical orientation (Matarazzo & Patterson, 1986). What is needed but unavailable is an approach to brief therapy compatible with all theoretical orientations.

The problems just described apply to practitioners in general. In addition, special brief therapy training problems can occur in certain clinic and graduate training settings. Organizations such as HMOs (Health Maintenance Organizations), managed care clinics, and CMHCs (Community Mental Health Centers) often encourage or require brief treatment within their settings. Typically such settings have employees who have been trained primarily as traditional (time-unlimited) therapists and need training in treatment abbreviation. These professionals usually represent a range of theoretical orientations so that brief therapy training in a single orientation-based approach will not be acceptable to all. At the same time, it is often desirable for a setting to have some consistency in its approach to brief therapy for training, supervising, and administrative purposes. A common but less than optimal solution is for the setting to encourage a particular brief therapy approach (and its conceptual/theoretical baggage), often augmented by a workshop, reading, or video training. Unfortunately, those clinicians from a theoretical framework other than the trainer's may gain little from such training (Backer, Liberman, & Keuhnel, 1986).

Similar problems exist in the training of student psychotherapists. It is common wisdom and strategy to train students in traditional therapy before brief therapy (Baldwin, 1977; Budman & Gurman, 1988), so a diversity of theoretical orientations is often established among students before brief therapy training occurs. This can lead to the theory incompatibility problems described earlier: it may be quite difficult to find a training resource with a theoretical base broad enough to accommodate a wide range of treatment approaches. In any case, brief therapy books present techniques and conceptualization that may be inappropriately narrow (or confusingly eclectic) for students in training. It is difficult enough for students to master a primary theory and associated techniques without having to accommodate a less than completely compatible brief therapy theory and techniques.

The problems resulting from the link between theory and brief therapy technique are unnecessary if one makes a distinction between psychotherapeutic treatment techniques and the format in which they are delivered. Although the behavior and cognitive change techniques of brief therapy are as variable as the many theories from which they derive, the procedures and strategies of *abbreviating* treatment are similar for all approaches to brief therapy. Brief therapy can be done with almost any theory of psychopathology and affiliated treatment techniques by adapting these to a briefer format. The uniqueness of brief therapy centers around strategies for abbreviation of treatment focus, scope, and goals rather than theory of problems or techniques of behavior change.

Affiliation of brief therapy technique with any particular treatment approach is unnecessary. This becomes obvious as one considers the very wide range of schools associated with brief therapy and the positive impact achieved by many different approaches (Shapiro & Shapiro, 1982; Smith, Glass, & Miller, 1980; Wierzbicki, 1993). Since most treatment orientations are compatible with brief therapy, teaching a new theoretical orientation along with the skills of treatment abbreviation unnecessarily complicates the latter task.

This book presents an approach to brief therapy training that can be used by therapists from almost every theoretical orientation. The methods employed encourage *practicing therapists* to retain their preferred theoretical orientation and therapy style; it provides a framework for adapting one's preferred treatment approach to a brief format. The emphasis is on adapting treatment to a brief format rather than teaching new therapy techniques or theory. For those *graduate students* who are still exploring different orientations, it encourages them to select their orientation independent of brief therapy considerations. The thesis of this book is that effective brief therapy can be done by therapists from almost every orientation and that therapy is done best when therapists work from within their preferred school and style. In short, this book describes an approach to brief therapy compatible with virtually all theoretical orientations. It does not represent a school of therapy but simply a strategy for abbreviating most approaches to treatment.

The eclecticism in this book is not achieved by denying the importance of theory or even by adopting the currently popular, diplomatic viewpoint that all schools of therapy are equally effective. It is achieved by acknowledging that most of the published approaches to brief therapy share many common elements and that these elements can be adapted to almost any school of therapy. The text emphasizes training of skills relevant to these common elements.

Besides being compatible with a wide range of theoretical orientations, the strategy presented is also compatible with the wide range of treatment durations prescribed by the various approaches to brief therapy. Most approaches prescribe about eight to 20 sessions, but some prescribe only one or two and others as many as 40 sessions. Because the same basic abbreviating strategies are used regardless of prescribed duration, the general approach recommended in this book can be used for brief treatments of a wide range of durations. Special acknowledgment is made of applications to very brief (one to four sessions) therapy because some settings restrict treatment to such a duration and many clients terminate after only a few sessions.

These procedures have been "field tested" by the author with hundreds of therapists from diverse orientations in CMHC, managed care, private practice, and both masters and doctoral level graduate school settings. The impact of the training on therapists *and clients* has been evaluated and found to increase the use of brief therapy, improve client satisfaction, and improve some aspects of treatment outcome (Pekarik, 1994).

While the special strategies associated with brief therapy are important, they may be less important than the motive to do brief therapy. Much of what is done in brief therapy is a fairly straightforward adaptation of traditional therapy skills and is not especially difficult to master. The *desire* to do brief therapy, an understanding of its effects, and an enthusiasm for exploiting its potential seem to be important prerequisites for doing effective brief therapy, however. A grudging acceptance of clinic or third-party payers' policies is probably not conducive to good brief therapy. It is the author's conviction that psychotherapy research provides a very strong rationale for doing brief therapy independent of the cost-containment forces that have recently emerged, that is, there are strong humanitarian and ethical rationales for doing brief therapy. Because of this, a thorough rationale for brief therapy based on psychotherapy process and outcome research is presented before the introduction of techniques in this book. The material presented in Chapter Two outlines brief therapy's potential for better serving most clients, provides a pragmatic foundation for the use of brief therapy with a wide range of clients, and describes the research findings on which the brief therapy strategies described later are based. Broadly speaking, Chapter Two provides an empirical basis for abbreviating treatment. Chapter Three addresses the complex set of practical, ethical, and humanitarian issues involved in selecting cases for which brief therapy is most appropriate. Chapter Four presents a theoretical model and philosophical foundation for a particular transtheoretical approach to brief therapy, while Chapters Five through Nine describe the techniques of how to abbreviate treatment. Throughout that latter section, a simulated case study is used to illustrate each abbreviating technique after it is described. Because the same case is used throughout the text, the case examples presented throughout the chapters collectively represents a thorough case study that illustrates the abbreviating strategies recommended in the text. A session-by-session description of a more difficult brief therapy case is provided in Appendix A. Finally, special practice issues associated with brief therapy are discussed in Chapter Ten. It is acknowledged that there are particular advantages as well as difficulties associated with brief therapy; organizational policy changes are recommended that may make it easier to do brief therapy.

Chapter One

Introduction

It is predicted that the great majority of future health and mental health services will be delivered through managed care, with costs contained through the use of prospective reimbursement (capitated payment), by the turn of the century (Cummings, 1995; Frank & Vandenbos, 1994; Weiner, 1994). This virtually guarantees that mental health services, including outpatient psychotherapy, will be brief for the majority of current and future clients. Under these circumstances, it is easy to lose sight of the fact that there are nonfiscal reasons to recommend the use of brief therapy. *Before* the current wave of cost containment, that is, between the late 1960s and mid-1980s, several authors (including myself) advocated increased use of brief therapy based on client preference, treatment outcome, and treatment attrition pattern research (for example, Baldwin, 1977; Bellak & Small, 1978; Bloom, 1979, 1984; Budman & Gurman, 1983; Miller & Hester, 1986; Pekarik, 1985; Stone & Crowthers, 1972; Straker, 1968). It is that basically humanitarian and client-oriented view that prompted the development of the treatment abbreviation procedures described in this book.

Unfortunately, the current cost-containment policies that have "popularized" brief treatment in recent years often mandate it for all clients regardless of individual clinical needs. This has understandably resulted in concerns about inadequate care, denial of care, and associated ethical dilemmas that might result from managed, abbreviated treatment (Newman & Bricklin, 1991). The association of brief treatment with new and sometimes coercive delivery policies has yielded a host of fiscal, political, and professional role issues for mental health professionals who now increasingly find themselves in a state of dislocation and disorganization. In such a climate it is important, though difficult, to distinguish the brief approach to treatment from the policies that mandate its use. Most advocates of brief therapy recommend that psychotherapists retain autonomy and flexibility regarding prescription of treatment duration. My advocacy of this position is clear throughout this book, though the strategies I describe can also be used when treatment duration is capped by clinic or corporate policy.

The stresses of the current delivery climate make it difficult for many professionals to consider the potential benefits of brief therapy; ironically, it was easier to argue for a humanitarian justification of brief therapy before its current "popularity." A description of my own development of interest in brief therapy may help explain why I advocate its use with many clients independent of (perhaps in spite of) contemporary managed care policies. My interest in brief therapy initially grew out of my work with treatment dropouts. As a clinical administrator at a mental health center in the late 1970s, I was alarmed at the early attrition and high dropout rates from treatment. As this concern evolved into a research interest, I studied dropout rates, treatment outcome for dropouts, and client reasons for dropping out. From interviews and surveys of clients, it became apparent that clients preferred treatment that was at variance with the preferences of most therapists: they wanted treatment that was problem rather than personality-oriented, modest in scope, and brief. These of course are the hallmarks of brief therapy. Inspired by my own research with dropouts as well as others' research that suggested that treatment abbreviation is associated with lowered dropout rates (Straker, 1968; Sledge et al., 1990), I explored the use of brief therapy as a means of increasing treatment satisfaction and reducing dropout (Pekarik, 1988, 1990, 1994). At about the same time, I took a part-time position at a managed care (staff model) clinic in order to gain further experience doing brief therapy and monitoring its effects. This clinic was well-run, well-staffed, and provided clinicians some flexibility regarding treatment duration. These research and clinical experiences have convinced me that brief therapy can be a consumer-oriented treatment that best serves most (though not all) clients. It has many advantages: it is compatible with client preferences, has good outcome and client satisfaction, and its efficiency makes brief treatment potentially more accessible than longer treatment. These claims for the advantages of brief therapy for clients will be further discussed in detail in Chapter Two.

The reader is reminded that what is being advocated is a treatment strategy and philosophy, *not* a service delivery system (e.g., a particular managed care service). There are many consumer pitfalls when treatment is abbreviated (or extended) for a profit motive. Each type of service delivery format should have consumer safeguards identified. Further elaboration of ethical issues associated with treatment abbreviation and treatment extension is presented throughout this book. Interested readers are also referred to others who have addressed ethical issues involved in treatment abbreviation and extension, such as Haas and Cummings (1991) and Newman and Bricklin (1991).

HISTORICAL, THEORETICAL, AND TECHNICAL FOUNDATIONS OF BRIEF THERAPY

There are dozens of approaches to brief therapy, each using either a mainstream theory of problem determination (psychopathology) or its own derivative micro-theory and associated treatment techniques. Most share certain features described later in this chapter. All are sensitive to treatment duration. For ease of discussion, "brief therapy" will be used in this section to denote the admittedly diverse group of therapies that share time sensitivity as an important issue. In this section, a brief review of the foundation of brief therapy is provided for two important reasons. The first is to further remind the reader that brief therapy is not something derived from managed care, but a set of treatment strategies with a diverse and complex history. The second reason is to identify the particular foundations of the transtheoretical approach to treatment abbreviation described in this book.

Brief therapy has a history as long as psychotherapy itself. Several authors have documented that abbreviated versions of standard psychotherapy have always existed, and that even Freud occasionally did treatment in just a few sessions (Bloom, 1992; Budman & Gurman, 1988; Koss & Butcher, 1986). A great many authors have contributed theory or technique to brief therapy in the past one hundred years. However, I regard four particular developments as especially important contributors to modern brief therapies: the development of crisis intervention, beginning with Lindemann's work in the 1940s; the evolution of cognitive-behavioral approaches and the empirical support for their efficacy; the evolution of modern psychodynamic theorizing (such as E. Erikson's) and the associated adaptation of psychodynamic treatment to a brief format; and the community mental health movement.

Lindemann's (1944) development of crisis intervention, later elaborated by Caplan (1963), provided important theoretical and technical contributions to contemporary brief therapy. Most important was the theoretical contribution. Lindemann's treatment derived from counseling the grieving survivors and relatives of the deceased of the Coconut Grove nightclub fire in 1942, that killed 493 people. He (a) identified general and *predictable* emotional and physical patterns of responses among those he treated and (b) focused his work on reactions to the *event* of the tragedy. These were two critical steps that diverged from traditional emphasis on *personality* in cases of emotional upset. Lindemann found that certain clinical strategies, such as the facilitation of the expression of grief, were helpful with a wide range of clients, regardless of their particular personalities. Lindemann later used the same logic to conjecture that other kinds of life crises (e.g., residential relocation associated with "urban renewal") might likewise perpetuate predictable maladaptive behavior, and created standard procedures for helpers to use in order to treat and prevent problems associated with the crises. Stressful scenarios to which he or others applied his crisis intervention strategy included death or suicide of a family member, retirement, school entry, premature birth, and psychiatric hospitalization of a family member (Bloom, 1984).

Caplan (1964, 1963) later extended this thinking to create a general theory of crisis development that encompassed a wide range of potential life crises; he defined crisis in terms of stress, coping behaviors, and resources rather than a limited list of particular situations. This allowed for an extremely wide range of problems for which clients seek psychotherapy to be conceptualized as life crises. He also developed a general strategy for assisting those in a crisis that focused on therapist accessibility, family and therapist support, coping with the current problem situation, the provision of information, and use of community resources.

Lindemann's and Caplan's efforts were very important in providing a theoretical foundation and clinical strategies that were usable by psychotherapists from many different theoretical orientations—one of their great contributions was that no particular school of therapy was required for use of their strategies. But the application of their contributions was restricted by their times: crisis intervention (and more generally, other brief therapies) was generally seen as a relatively minor adjunct to standard psychotherapy, considered the far more powerful, sophisticated, and preferred treatment. Bloom (1984, 1992) and Baldwin (1977) have provided excellent descriptions of the profound and pervasive bias that psychotherapists traditionally have had for longer treatments. Crisis intervention, then, was restricted to a narrow set of clinical conditions and was commonly a prelude to long-term therapy. It was not regarded as a sufficient treatment of psychopathology.

The behavioral and cognitive therapies that emerged in the 1950s to 1960s were briefer alternatives to traditional therapy that *were* vigorously promoted as *sufficient* means of treating mental disorders and emotional upsets. These therapies provided theory, technique, and empirical support for the effectiveness of treatments that were brie*fer* than the prevailing alternative approaches. A good case can be made that cognitive-behavioral approaches, although briefer than early traditional therapies, should not be considered to always be brief therapy for both philosophical and empirical (i.e., these therapies are frequently *not* brief) reasons. I have dealt extensively with this issue in Chapter Two. Nevertheless, cognitive-behaviorists have always touted the relative efficiency of their approach compared to longer, especially psychodynamic therapies (and have therefore contributed to treatment abbreviation). More important, cognitive-behavior therapists have been the primary instigators and publishers of psychotherapy outcome research and have relied heavily on brief versions of their therapies in these studies (Shapiro & Shapiro, 1982; Lambert & Bergin, 1994). Budman and Gurman (1988) have made the point that the published formal evaluation of psychotherapy is really reducible to the formal evaluation of *brief* psychotherapy, since the great majority of published outcome research has relied on brief treatments. Because most of these reports have relied on cognitive-behavioral treatments, we can further state that the therapy outcome literature is primarily an assessment of *brief cognitive-behavioral* therapies. One of the main contributions of cognitive-behavioral researchers is that they have thoroughly demonstrated that relatively brief therapy can be effective.

Because cognitive-behavioral techniques are routinely highly operationalized (their procedures are clearly specified), they can be adapted for brief therapy use by therapists from many orientations. As a result, many brief therapy approaches outside of the cognitive-behavioral orientation have adopted such techniques. This development of techniques amenable to a brief format is an important contribution of cognitive-behavioral therapy to treatment abbreviation.

By the late 1960s, then, the crisis interventions and cognitive-behavioral fields provided theory, technique, philosophy, and empirically-based credibility for treatments briefer than the standard psychotherapy of that era. The community mental health movement (as expressed through the Community Mental Health Centers Act of 1963 and subsequent related legislation) gave clinicians an external set of inducements to abbreviate treatment and a compatible setting where briefer treatment was appropriate and needed. Several aspects of community mental health legislation and policies especially encouraged the use of abbreviated treatments. There was, of course, the mandate to serve the entire community—an emphasis on treatment accessibility. The long waiting lists common to many centers encouraged the use of brief outpatient and inpatient treatment as a means of accommodating the high demand for service. Community Mental Health Centers (CMHCs) also created a new psychotherapy clientele—middle to lower class clients who previously could not afford mental health treatment (this "downward" extension of mental health treatment was further perpetuated by third-party payers' wide-scale inclusion of reimbursement for mental health services beginning in the 1970s). Brief therapy was often seen as the most appropriate treatment for the new lower class clients. Social class has been found to be consistently associated with treatment duration (Garfield, 1994; Wierzbicki & Pekarik,

1993). There were other features that encouraged brief treatment as well. All federally funded CMHC's were required to provide 24 hour emergency services and widely adopted crisis intervention for this purpose. And lastly, the thousands of CMHC clinicians were *salaried* employees who, unlike private practitioners, had no financial incentive to do long-term treatment. While many of the CMHC psychotherapists still preferred and attempted to deliver long-term therapy, they generally failed to do so: the average CMHC client attended fewer than five sessions (see Chapter Two for elaborate documentation of these assertions). At the very least, the CMHC movement introduced a generation of therapists to the experience of treatment being brief.

By the early 1970s, then, there were broad and pervasive influences to abbreviate treatment: theory, technique, empirical outcome validation, public policy, and demonstrated practical needs were all present in forms that were conducive to treatment abbreviation. It is not surprising that the major traditional long-term approach to treatment–psychodynamic therapy–began to be adapted to a brief format on a wide scale at about that time (for example, the works of Balint, Ornstein, & Balint, 1972; Bellak & Small, 1965; Davanloo, 1978; Malan, 1973, 1976; Mann, 1973; Sifneos, 1972; and Wolberg, 1980). The broader zeitgeist, along with the availability of compatible neo-analytic theorizing that emphasized the prospect of adult development (e.g., Erikson, 1959) has resulted in continued development of psychodynamic brief therapies. They are a very important source of abbreviating theory and technique, and have provided some of the most demonstrably effective (e.g., Klerman et al., 1984) and radically brief (e.g., Bloom, 1992; Talmon, 1990) approaches available. The continued development of brief psychodynamic and cognitive-behavioral approaches, along with a growing effort toward theory and technique integration (Stricker & Gold, 1993) probably bodes well for the future refinement of brief therapy.

Psychodynamic and cognitive-behavioral approaches have been conspicuous but certainly not the sole contributors to treatment abbreviation. Family and marital therapies (Epstein et al., 1990) and strategic approaches (Rosenbaum, 1990) are compatible with and have made major contributions to brief therapy. As brief therapy texts illustrate, contributions are currently being made by almost all theoretical orientations (Wells & Giannetti, 1990; Zeig & Gilligan, 1990).

In summary, a solid theoretical and technical foundation for brief therapy has been developed over the past several decades. As shown in Chapter Two, there are also sound empirical, pragmatic, and philosophical bases for doing brief treatment. But it is the increased financial management of health care necessitated by its high cost that is by far the greatest force contributing to current treatment abbreviation efforts. Just a few years ago a brief therapy text would require an elaborate section on the then-increasing management of mental health care as one justification for learning to do brief therapy. Treatment restrictions are now so widespread that they have become a routine part of treatment planning–abbreviated treatment is now standard treatment. This pragmatic influence will undoubtedly continue with or without federal health care reform initiatives.

ELEMENTS COMMON TO MOST BRIEF THERAPIES

A small sampling of the diversity of brief therapy approaches was presented in the previous section. The trend among authors of brief therapy approaches is to develop a unique theory of human problems and an associated set of somewhat unique treatment techniques. Since authors of the various brief therapies make little attempt to coordinate their efforts, the field has been presented with a confusing diversity of therapies. Even within a general theoretical category there is great variation. For example, consider that within a broadly psychodynamic orientation there are many distinct approaches to brief therapy, each with a very different conceptual emphasis: Klerman (Klerman et al., 1984) focuses on interpersonal relationships, Lewin (1970) on the superego and parental introjection, Sifneos (1987) on anxiety, Bellak (1984) on the link between current symptoms and remote historical antecedents, and Wolberg (1980) on a combination of concepts from traditional analytic, learning, and other theories. It seems that an understanding of the effectiveness of the many different brief therapies cannot be explained by any one theory. This makes it difficult to understand brief therapy's general effectiveness (across theories). Saving this situation from strategic and technical chaos is the fact that close inspection finds abbreviating strategies *common* to most brief therapy approaches despite their theoretical diversity. A number of authors have made this observation (Bloom, 1992; Budman & Gurman, 1988; Koss & Butcher, 1986; Koss & Shiang, 1994; Pekarik, 1990, 1994). Common elements cited by most of these authors include:

- a limited but flexible use of time
- a clear, specific treatment focus
- limited goals negotiated with the client
- a focus on present stress
- rapid assessment
- a high level of therapist and client activity
- eclectic use of techniques

The key to understanding effective brief treatment lies within these elements.

GENERAL ABBREVIATION STRATEGIES: INTRODUCTION TO A MODEL

The basic approach of this text is to describe how these general treatment abbreviation strategies can be used from within almost any theoretical orientation, so that any therapist can abbreviate his or her preferred way of treating clients to a brief format. A model for treatment abbreviation based on the common abbreviating strategies is presented in detail in Chapter Four.

There are many potential benefits to this approach. First and foremost, it allows a psychotherapist to retain one's current theoretical orientation and set of therapy techniques. Not only is this easier than learning a totally new approach, it may be by far more effective: research suggests that clinicians benefit little from training provided in the context of a foreign theoretical orientation (Matarazzo & Patterson, 1986). A second benefit is that, by using a generic psychotherapy language, it is relatively easy to use this approach in training settings where there are diverse orientations (e.g., most clinics, graduate schools, and workshops). This is one of the few approaches that has been demonstrated to increase the use of brief therapy and improve treatment impact when used with a diversity of therapists in standard clinic settings (Pekarik, 1994).

Descriptions of technique, strategy, and other practical matters make up the bulk of this book. But research has demonstrated that therapist attitude is as important as technique for conducting effective brief treatment: acceptance of brief therapy's rationale and philosophy is associated with its effectiveness (Burlingame, et al., 1989; Koss & Shiang, 1994). For that reason, extensive description of brief therapy's rationale is presented in the next chapter and related philosophy and values are emphasized in Chapter Four. The rationale presented in Chapter Two is primarily an empirical one, based on research that addresses client treatment preferences, actual attendance patterns, and the relationship of treatment duration to client satisfaction, outcome, and compliance. In the course of addressing brief therapy's effectiveness, the broader nature of psychotherapy and the determinants of its effectiveness are also addressed. This effort to understand brief therapy in the larger context of psychotherapy is extended throughout this book, with special attention to it in Chapter Three (client selection), Four (a conceptual model of brief treatment), and Ten (special practice issues associated with brief therapy). It is hoped that a thorough presentation of brief therapy will provide a greater understanding of psychotherapy in general.

Chapter Two

Rationale

Very often the rationale for doing brief therapy is that third-party payers or some other cost-containment contingency require it. This is unlikely to be acceptable to most clinicians, especially given the traditional premium placed on long-term treatment (Bloom, 1992). There are alternative reasons for considering the use of brief therapy, but these derive from research literature not widely read by clinicians. The purpose of this chapter is to acquaint the reader with the relevant literature.

This chapter reviews key areas of psychotherapy research relevant to the issue of brief therapy utility. Four areas are emphasized: (1) client treatment preferences; (2) actual attendance patterns in standard practice settings; (3) determinants and effects of psychotherapy dropout; and (4) the relationship of treatment duration to outcome and satisfaction. In this and the following chapter, pragmatic and ethical implications of these issues will be addressed, providing both a rationale for the use of brief therapy and delineation of the circumstances under which its use is most supportable.

CLIENT EXPECTATIONS AND PREFERENCES REGARDING TREATMENT LENGTH, CONTENT, AND GOALS

Treatment Length

The great majority of clients expect therapy to be brief, an expectation that long antedates brief therapy's current popularity. Pre-

---

Material in this chapter was previously published in *Handbook of Effective Psychotherapy*, Thomas R. Giles (Ed.). Plenum Press, 1993.

therapy surveys of clients consistently find that over 70 percent expect treatment to consist of ten visits or less and about half expect five or fewer visits (Garfield & Wolpin, 1963; Pekarik, 1991a; Pekarik & Wierzbicki, 1986). Clients at a managed mental health care setting expected even briefer treatment: 88 percent expected five or fewer visits (Pekarik, 1991b). In a study that distinguished expectations from preferences, McGreevy (1987) found that 62 percent of college undergraduates expected psychotherapy to be 10 or fewer visits, but 79 percent preferred it that short. These expectations are probably influenced by client experiences with general health care, where the average citizen has a total of two to three 15 minute outpatient visits per year (National Center for Health Statistics, 1988).

Client expectations for brief treatment run counter to therapist preferences for treatment duration. Therapy textbooks provide information on such duration prescriptions. Lambert, Shapiro, and Bergin (1986) represent the psychotherapy establishment with their reference to improvement after 26 sessions as an effect "that occurs in a relatively short period of time" (pg. 162). Of mainstream delivery of behavior therapy, considered a relatively short-term treatment, Wilson (1981) acknowledged that "therapy lasting from 25 to 50 sessions is commonplace" (pg. 141) and Norcross and Wogan's (1983) survey of members of the Association for the Advancement of Behavior Therapy found that only about one-fourth of their clients were estimated to terminate in less than three months of treatment. These references are representative of commonly accepted views of the length of standard contemporary psychotherapies. Further indication of treatment duration prescriptions can be found in therapy technique texts. Corsini's (1991) book is representative; in it, prescribed durations for a fictitious case example range from 19 to 32 sessions. The case example is of a *normal* person with minor though persistent problems.

In order to identify mainstream contemporary prescriptions of *brief* treatment, recently published texts that each described several approaches to brief therapy were consulted (Wells & Giannetti, 1990; Zeig & Gilligan, 1990). These identify the lower limits of treatment duration prescribed by experts. Generally, the recommendations were for either ten to 20 or 20 to 30 sessions for the more than 20 popular brief therapy approaches described, duration prescriptions considerably longer than the ten sessions or less expected by clients.

In one of the very few surveys of practitioners' preferences, Pekarik and Finney-Owen (1987) asked 165 CMHC therapists to indicate the length of treatment they preferred for most clients: 77 percent selected 11 or more sessions. The modal preference in these public settings (generally regarded as short-term oriented) was 11 to 20 sessions.

It is clear from the literature that clients expect and prefer a treatment course that is considerably briefer than that preferred by psychotherapists, most brief therapists, and practitioners in public clinics.

Treatment Content and Goals

Not surprisingly, clients' expectations and preferences for treatment content and goals are compatible with their ideas on treatment length, i.e., they have modest, pragmatic aspirations for both treatment length and goals. Studies generally find that clients expect a high level of direct advice, concrete problem definition, problem-solving, and therapist activity (e.g., Benbenishty & Schul, 1987; Hornstra et al., 1972; Llewelyn, 1988; Overall & Aronson, 1962; Pekarik & Wierzbicki, 1986). Therapists prefer less of the treatment characteristics just identified than clients do, more extensive treatment, personality rather than problem change, and more insight and feeling expression (Benbenishty & Schul, 1987; Hornstra et al., 1972; Llewelyn, 1988; Pekarik, 1985b). Not surprisingly, Overall and Aronson (1962) found that clients' expectations regarding treatment directives and early problem-solving usually were not met.

Research on treatment dropouts also suggests that many clients have modest, problem-focused treatment goals. Baekeland and Lundwall's (1975) dropout literature review concluded that many clients attend therapy until acute crises subside, then terminate. This suggests that clients seek crisis relief as a primary treatment goal. Surveys of dropouts consistently find that perceived improvement is one of the most common reasons given for dropping out (Acosta, 1980; Garfield, 1963; Pekarik, 1983b, 1992b). Pekarik (1983b, 1992) found that the dropouts who cited problem improvement as a dropout reason did, as a group, improve significantly based on intake and follow-up symptom inventory scores. These findings are consistent with the broader medical treatment literature that consistently finds symptom abatement as one of the primary reasons for treatment noncompliance (Dunbar & Agras, 1980).

Further evidence of therapists' preference for more ambitious treatment is found in the extensive literature devoted to preparing clients for psychotherapy (reviewed by Heitler, 1976); the preparation usually consists of correction of clients' expectation for immediate, direct help and indoctrination into the therapy subculture's ethic of longer treatment and ambitious goals (see Bloom, 1992 for elaboration of the latter issue).

ACTUAL TREATMENT ATTENDANCE PATTERNS

In the real world of both public clinic and private practice settings, treatment is typically very brief and much more in line with client than therapist preferences. This very brief treatment is sometimes by design but often by default, due to premature termination.

The mean number of sessions attended by CMHC outpatients is about five (National Institute of Mental Health, 1981). This finding was based on a survey of the universe of all federally funded CMHCs. Incredibly, this often-cited statistic is an exaggeration of the actual treatment duration since it is distorted by the few clients who attend very high numbers of sessions. The median is a more appropriate measure: it is about three and a half sessions (National Institute of Mental Health, 1979; Rosenstein & Milazzo-Sayre, 1981). Rosenstein and Milazzo-Sayre's (1981) report, based on a sample of over 1500 clinics, found that 63 percent of clients terminated *before* their fifth session and 75 percent terminated before the seventh session. The great majority of early terminators have the same sorts of disorders (Rosenstein & Milazzo-Sayre, 1981) and problem severity (Pekarik, 1983a, 1992) as outpatients in general. There is no client (diagnostic or demographic) subgroup for which the majority of clients attend more than ten sessions at public settings.

Private setting treatment duration is longer than public setting, but still extremely brief. Taube, Burns, and Kessler (1984) reported a mean number of private practice sessions of about 12 and a median of about four and a half. The modal number of sessions in both public and private clinic samples was one. About 44 percent of the private practice clients terminated before the fourth session and about 64 percent before the tenth. Other surveys of private practices have also found that less than half their clients attend more than ten to 15 sessions (Knesper, Pagnucco, & Wheeler, 1985; Koss, 1979; Pekarik, 1995). As in public clinics, the early terminating majority of clients are representative of the demographics and diagnoses of all clients at private settings–they include the severe and pervasive disorders.

The foregoing studies are typical of reports of treatment duration in public and private settings. It is most likely that they, if anything, are overestimates of current treatment duration, since the recent policy of third-party payers is to increasingly restrict the number of reimbursable outpatient sessions (Kiesler & Morton, 1988). In any case, more recent reports of treatment in standard practice settings (e.g., Weisz & Weiss, 1989) indicate continued very brief treatment. Interestingly, therapists seem to be quite unaware of the briefness of therapy in their own caseloads, overestimating actual treatment duration (Pekarik & Finney-Owen, 1987; Pekarik, 1993). The reason for this perceptual distortion is understandable: therapists are most aware of those clients with whom they spend the most time. And most of their time is spent with the small proportion of clients who attend many sessions. For example, Taube et al. (1984) found that private practitioners spent 65 percent of their therapy hours with the 17 percent of clients who attended 25 or more sessions, but only 4.7 percent of their time with the 43 percent of clients who attended one to three visits.

In summary, it is clear that treatment in standard practice public and private settings ends up being far briefer (for the great majority of clients) than the typical prescription and preferences of almost all therapists; this holds for standard therapy, behavioral and cognitive-behavioral therapy, and even most brief therapies. The great majority of clients do not receive anywhere near the "dose" of treatment widely assumed necessary and for which treatment is designed. To review: *Only about 14 percent of public clinic and 36 percent of private clients attend even brief therapy's minimum prescription of ten visits,* much less than the 20 visit minimum of more commonly prescribed treatment. To put this another way—mainstream therapies are compatible with the treatment courses of only a small minority of the clients who seek assistance. This seems reason enough to consider extensive training and application of brief therapy: it better matches actual treatment duration than standard treatment.

Premature Termination

Rates

Considering the steep attrition curve from outpatient psychotherapy, it is not surprising that a large percentage of cases are considered premature terminations by therapists. Reviews of dropout research generally find that about 50 percent of clients are considered dropouts (Baekeland & Lundwall, 1975; Wierzbicki & Pekarik, 1993). A report from the universe of federally funded CMHCs found similarly high dropout rates (National Institute of Mental Health, 1981).

Virtually nothing is known about private practice dropout rates, unfortunately. The best estimate is that they parallel the findings of attrition in public vs. private settings, i.e., dropout rates are probably lower in private settings but, given the great disparity between prescribed and actual treatment duration, a significant percentage of private clients probably drop out of treatment also.

Effects

Although hundreds of archival studies have addressed the dropout problem, very few have addressed the most salient aspect of dropouts, their treatment outcome. Garfield (1986, pg. 232) concluded that, "Detailed evaluations of the outcome of early terminators have not been made." Until recently, dropouts were not even routinely identified or their outcome reported in outcome research. It is almost as if therapists are unaware that dropouts and early terminators exist when it comes to prescribing, devising, and evaluating outcome of treatment.

The few studies that have reported the posttreatment adjustment of dropouts consistently find that clients who dropped out after a visit or two have poor outcome while those who drop out later have better outcome, in some cases similar to treatment completers (Pekarik, 1986). So while all dropouts are not treatment failures, many are.

In addition to the treatment outcome consideration, there are administrative, therapist morale, and fiscal problems posed by dropouts (Pekarik, 1985a). Premature termination is also consistently related to lower client satisfaction with treatment (Lebow, 1982).

Causes

There is no single simple cause of dropout or early termination. Literature reviews have found virtually no single client or therapist variable that is strongly and consistently related to dropout (Baekeland & Lundwall, 1975; Pekarik, 1985a; Wierzbicki & Pekarik, 1993). Stronger relationships have been found between dropout and more complex therapist-client interactions, (Duehn & Proctor, 1977; Epperson, Bushway, & Warman, 1983; Pekarik, 1988) and client expectations regarding treatment length (Pekarik, 1991a; Pekarik & Wierzbicki, 1986). Given the finding that any major discrepancy between treatment expectation and actual treatment content contributes to increased dropout (Horenstein & Houston, 1976), it is highly probable that the discrepancy between client and therapist expectations regarding treatment length, goals, and content cited earlier contributes to dropout rates.

The investigation of noncompliance with medical treatment, an issue very similar to mental health dropout, has found some very clear-cut results that are applicable to the dropout phenomenon. Reviewers of this literature consistently report that aspects of the treatment regimen and symptom abatement are the most important determinants of noncompliance. Specifically, long treatment duration, high treatment cost (in money, discomfort, or inconvenience), treatment complexity, and reduction of symptoms are strongly and consistently associated with noncompliance (Blackwell, 1976; Dunbar & Agras, 1980; Houpt et al., 1979). Psychotherapy dropouts also consistently have cited symptom abatement and dislike of the treatment regimen or therapist as two of their top three dropout reasons; practical problems such as transportation and cost was the third (Acosta, 1980; Garfield, 1963; Pekarik, 1983b, 1992b). Relative to most health care, psychotherapy designed for even ten to 20 visits is high in cost (in money, time, and inconvenience), complex, and results in its greatest impact (symptom abatement) long before its prescribed termination point (Pekarik, 1993). In other words, standard psychotherapy has all the ingredients for noncompliance.

In summary, psychotherapy dropout rates are quite high but entirely understandable given therapy's high cost, long duration, and the discrepancy between prescribed and actual treatment duration. Dropout rates are a major obstacle to the delivery of treatment and are associated with outcome, satisfaction, fiscal, administrative, and therapist morale problems. Very few studies have addressed treatment outcome for dropouts or ways to reduce dropout rates (Pekarik, 1985a, 1986). Of the latter, the major strategy has been to do "pre-therapy preparation" of clients, i.e., to indoctrinate them in the need to attend treatment as prescribed by therapists. Almost no suggestion is given to *altering the nature of the treatment* that seems to inevitably lead to high dropout rates. Those few studies that investigated the relationship of treatment duration to dropout rates have found that abbreviating treatment reduces dropout (Pekarik, 1988; Straker, 1968; Sledge et al., 1990). This impact on dropout reduction applies even to very low session dropouts–those with the worst follow-up adjustment.

RELATIONSHIP OF TREATMENT DURATION TO OUTCOME AND SATISFACTION

The foregoing sections show that clients expect and prefer treatment that has many of the characteristics of brief therapy–treatment that is brief and has low cost, a narrow focus, and modest goals. Furthermore, the great majority of clients actually attend treatment for only a brief duration. These are powerful arguments for considering brief therapy, but there has been a traditional counter-argument: that brief therapy is not as good as longer therapy. Clients' brief treatment preferences are often criticized as a naive "Band-Aid" approach to problems that are deep, have taken years to develop, and will take months to overcome. This criticism rests on the assumption that psychotherapy can and should address (a) the basic causes of problems and (b) all client problems. In traditional psychodynamic treatment this means addressing basic character (deep) rather than behavior (superficial) symptoms. Although not as obvious, other schools also make this "deeper/more superficial" dichotomy. For example, representing a cognitive-behavioral approach, Haaga and Davison (1986, pg. 261) state that social problem-solving training "seeks to teach a client a general procedure to use in solving problems, as opposed to alleviating only the client's most pressing problem. Goldfried (1980) noted that clients frequently enter therapy expecting rapid help in solving a particular problem, not generalized training . . . [In social problem-solving training] the client is a student learning a generally applicable self-control technique. . . ." While attempts to address the "deeper problems" (or even teach a general strategy rather than its application to a specific problem) are laudatory in the abstract, the reality of brief treatment durations precludes fixing deeper problems or general behavior patterns for most clients. Furthermore, this orientation denigrates the more modest goals likely to be preferred by the client. This denigration of the "Band-Aid" in favor of a more ambitious intervention would make sense if indeed little could be accomplished in a brief treatment and much more benefit were consistently delivered by longer treatment.

These are critical questions for brief therapy: is it beneficial and how does its outcome compare to longer treatment? The short answer to this is "Yes, it is beneficial and it compares quite favorably to longer treatment." The reader probably has some acquaintance with the outcome literature that supports brief therapy's efficacy. Nevertheless, there remains a strong ambivalence about brief therapy among many therapists undoubtedly influenced by a therapy subculture that idealizes longer, "deeper" treatment (Baldwin, 1979; Bloom, 1992) and a lack of awareness of the literature that addresses the relationship of treatment duration to outcome and client satisfaction. For these reasons the outcome literature is reviewed below.

Outpatient

Outcome for Time-Limited vs. Time-Unlimited Treatment

The relationship of treatment duration to outcome is addressed by several different research literatures. First and foremost are the studies that have randomly assigned clients to standard (time-unlimited) and brief (time-limited) treatment. There are enough such studies that they have been reviewed by several authors. The reviews of this literature all reach the same conclusion: There is no reliable overall difference in the effectiveness of time-limited and time-unlimited treatment (Bloom, 1984, 1992; Gurman & Kniskern, 1978; Koss & Butcher, 1986; Koss & Shiang, 1994; Luborsky, Singer, & Luborsky, 1975; Miller & Hester, 1986). The studies reviewed include investigations of individual, family, and child therapy and a wide range of visits in their comparison groups. For example, Piper et al. (1984) had brief therapy that averaged 22 visits and long therapy that averaged 76 visits, while Edwards et al. (1977) randomly assigned clients to either two sessions or a one-year treatment program. It is impressive that regardless of the client population studied, the duration of brief and long treatment, the theoretical orientation of the brief therapist, or the dependent measures of outcome, the brief treatments fared as well as the longer ones. A recent well-controlled outcome study of depressed clients has also supported this finding (Shapiro et al., 1994, 1995).

Comparisons Among Brief Treatments and No Treatment

There is a substantial body of research that has compared brief therapy to no therapy and has assessed the relative effectiveness of different types of brief treatments. Studies typically find improved functioning of the briefly treated groups relative to control groups (Koss & Butcher, 1986). Budman and Gurman (1988, pg. 7) make the cogent point that "virtually every major review of the efficacy of various individual therapies . . . has been an unacknowledged review" of brief therapy since the great majority of studies reviewed have assessed quite brief treatment. They note that two of the most widely cited meta-analyses of treatment outcome (Shapiro & Shapiro, 1982; Smith, Glass, & Miller, 1980) reviewed treatments that were very brief—the typical treatment reviewed by Shapiro and Shapiro was only seven hours. These analyses concluded that the brief treatments analyzed were significantly more effective than no treatment (all used some type of untreated control group).

Treatment Length and Outcome in Time-Unlimited Treatment

The one study that is most often cited as a defense of long-term treatment (Howard et al., 1986) upon critical inspection actually provides some support for short-term treatment. Howard et al. analyzed data from 15 studies of long-term treatment that assessed improvement at each visit. The studies Howard et al. review are not representative of standard practice, however: nine of the 15 studies had a median of ten or more visits, and seven had a median of 15 or more visits. These are far in excess of the CMHC median of three and a half visits (National Institute of Mental Health, 1981) and the private practice median of five (Taube, Burns, & Kessler, 1984). Settings were also unusual, with six of the 15 being university clinics. Therapists were also unrepresentative, in that they all had psychodynamic or "interpersonal" orientations.

The authors present data that shows continued improvement up through the twenty-sixth session and beyond. The improvement measures emphasized by the authors are based upon *therapist* ratings, however, and a substantial body of research has shown that therapist-rated measures of improvement are consistently biased in favor of long-term treatment when compared to behavioral measures and psychological tests (Johnson & Gelso, 1980). Howard et al.'s (1986) *client rated* measures of improvement present a different picture: with them the greatest improvement occurs in the first eight visits. The percentage of improved clients increased from 53 percent at eight visits to 60 percent at 26 visits, a very modest increase considering the time invested. This is consistent with Smith et al.'s (1980) meta-analyses that found most improvement to occur in the first six to eight sessions. Interestingly, Howard's more recent research has found that the majority of treatment impact occurs within early sessions on most measures (Howard et al., 1993).

Treatment Duration and Satisfaction

Several studies have assessed the relationship between treatment length and satisfaction. Reviews of this literature have concluded that treatment length is unrelated to client satisfaction with treatment (Bloom, 1984, 1992; Lebow, 1982).

Impact of Brief Therapy on Subsequent Medical Care Utilization

A substantial literature has shown that brief psychotherapy has been associated with subsequent lowered use of medical treatment

(Jones & Vischi, 1979; Mumford et al., 1984). Most dramatic in this literature are studies that show reduced medical care after a single psychotherapy visit. Cummings and Follette (Cummings, 1977a, 1977b; Cummings & Follette, 1968; Follette & Cummings, 1967) found this to be the case in a series of studies. One of the groups they studied was a group of 80 emotionally upset clients assigned to a single psychotherapy session. They found a dramatic and surprising outcome, that a single interview (with no subsequent psychotherapy) was associated with a 60 percent reduction in medical care use that was maintained over the entire five year follow-up period.

In a similar type of study, Rosen and Wiens (1979) found that clients who received only a single evaluation interview had a significant reduction in a wide range of medical care treatment, both outpatient and inpatient. The more recent analyses of studies of this type (e.g., Mumford et al., 1984) find reduced medical care utilization to be primarily inpatient care.

Impact of Very Brief (One to Two Session) Therapy

Data from diverse sources suggest that very brief (one or two visits) treatment may be effective for some outpatients. Edwards et al. (1977) randomly assigned alcohol abuse clients to either two conjoint sessions (client and spouse) or treatment options covering a variety of outpatient and inpatient services over a year's time. No significant differences were found between groups on any measure (including objective drinking measures and more subjective adjustment measures) at one and two year follow-up. In a series of studies, Miller (Miller, Gribskov, & Mortell, 1981; Miller & Taylor, 1980; Miller, Taylor, & West, 1980) randomly assigned alcohol abuse clients to either a structured one- to two- session treatment emphasizing self-directed treatment or longer treatment ranging from six to 18 visits. No outcome differences were found over the follow-up periods, which ranged from six to 24 months. Where employed, no-treatment control groups were less improved than treatment groups.

These impressive studies done by Edwards and Miller and their colleagues were the only ones found in the literature that comprehensively evaluated clients assigned to *planned* very brief treatment and longer treatment. A host of other studies suggest that very brief treatment may be effective, however. Bloom (1981, 1992) and Talmon (1990) both reported that a very large proportion of clients, about 90 percent, seen for planned one or two session treatment reported improvement at follow-up ranging from three to 12 months, and that most did not seek additional time-unlimited treatment though it was offered. These latter reports, unfortunately, suffer from relying on simple client reports; more research is needed on this topic.

Impromptu Very Brief Therapy

In addition to the foregoing studies of *planned* formal brief therapy, there is evidence that *unplanned* brief treatment (i.e., dropouts) and informal brief therapy (i.e., a brief course of treatment delivered by a therapist trained in and usually having a preference for longer-term treatment) of one to a few visits is often associated with positive treatment outcome. These studies are important because of the large percentage of clients in standard practice settings who terminate by default or after "informal" brief therapy (Budman & Gurman, 1988; Garfield, 1986). There are a number of "naturalistic" psychotherapy studies that have assessed the posttreatment adjustment of clients who have attended only a few outpatient sessions. Weisz & Weiss (1989) found that child outpatients who attended a single session with their parents were significantly improved at six and 12 month follow-up using a behavior checklist, focal problems identified by parents, and teacher reports as dependent measures. When compared with treatment completers (who averaged 12.4 visits), the single session groups were as much or more improved, depending on the measure and follow-up period.

Pekarik (1983a) assessed the posttreatment adjustment of very briefly (one to two session) treated adults using a symptom checklist at intake and three month follow-up. Overall, only a small percentage of early terminators were improved at follow-up. When the early terminators were divided between dropouts and completers, however, it was found that the very briefly treated completers were as improved as the completers who attended three or more sessions. Pekarik (1992a) and Pekarik and Tongier (1993) replicated this result with separate samples of outpatients. Getz et al. (1975), Gottschalk et al. (1967), and Silverman and Beech (1979) have reported that a majority of very briefly treated terminators were improved at follow-up.

All the studies just described employed fairly standard psychotherapy outcome criteria and are uniform in finding a substantial proportion of very briefly treated clients improved at follow-up. Those studies that employed the most rigorous research methods (Edwards et al., 1977; the Miller studies, and Weisz & Weiss, 1989) found that very brief and longer treatments had equal impact for the client groups examined.

Outpatient Summary

Several different outpatient literatures have been examined in order to assess the impact of brief treatment. All were consistent in finding clinical benefit associated with brief treatment and very little outcome difference was found between brief and longer treatments. While it is possible that this outcome similarity is attributable to weaknesses in the studies (i.e., a failure to detect actual differences), this is made unlikely by the variety and breadth of relevant research that was reviewed. In any case, the onus of demonstrating superiority of longer treatment is on those who would claim its superiority, and this has not been accomplished. At the very least, it is clear that brief treatments have positive impact and warrant use with some clients.

Inpatient

As with outpatient studies, there is substantial literature on comparisons of both mental health and alcohol inpatient treatments of varying lengths. Reviews of the mental health literature (Bloom, 1984, 1992; Miller & Hester, 1986; Riessman, Rabkin, & Struening, 1977) have concluded that, as with outpatient treatment, short-term inpatient treatment is as effective as long-term treatment. Like the outpatient studies, the lengths of stay vary among studies. The contrasted treatment lengths range from 11 vs. 60 days to 90 vs. 177 days. Regardless of contrasted length range, the briefer treatments fare as well as the longer ones.

After reviewing the inpatient alcohol and drug literature, Miller and Hester (1986) also concluded that there is virtually no overall difference in the impact of programs of varying lengths.

RELATIONSHIP OF CLIENT CHARACTERISTICS TO BRIEF THERAPY OUTCOME

The majority of individual studies cited by reviewers did not restrict brief therapy to select client subgroups, i.e., the results (equivalent benefits) reported are for the wide range of outpatients and inpatients. Koss and Butcher (1986) specifically addressed the issue of client characteristics and outcome in their review, and concluded that none of the client characteristics usually identified as a prerequisite for brief therapy success (behavior problem of acute onset, good previous adjustment, ability to relate, motivation) or any other characteristic was any more related to brief therapy outcome than to time-unlimited treatment outcome. While many brief therapy advocates recommend selecting only certain clients for brief therapy, there are almost no empirical grounds for such selection. Few clients would be excluded from brief therapy on purely empirical grounds. This leaves pragmatic and ethical issues to be considered in client selection, a topic further discussed in Chapter Three.

SUMMARY

Independent of cost-containment issues, several literatures give strong support for widespread application of brief therapy. There are three major justifications for its use. First, brief therapy possesses characteristics desired by most clients: they prefer brief, problem-focused treatment that aspires to modest goals. Second, a great majority of clients attend treatment for only a brief time, (though this brevity is often achieved by treatment dropout). The attrition rates are so uniform and pervasive across settings that it is virtually inevitable that a large majority of clients will terminate before their tenth visit in public and private settings. Skill in brief therapy allows provision of appropriate treatment for the majority of clients who terminate early. Third, outcome research consistently shows brief therapy to be as effective as time-unlimited treatment for a wide range of clients.

Research has *not* supported the notions that brief therapy is superficial, only effective with mild problems, or results in higher relapse rates. While future research may find that brief and longer-term therapies are especially well-suited to certain client subgroups, there is no empirical evidence for this at present. To the contrary, all evidence suggests that brief therapy is beneficial for a wide range of clients.

Chapter Three

Client Selection

The question of who should be treated in brief and longer therapy has always been of interest. In this era of increasingly mandated brief therapy, the selection issue might seem less important, since the nature of service delivery contracts and third-party payers' policies often dictate treatment duration. These conditions have resulted in greater interest than ever in selection issues, however, as ethical, legal, humanitarian, and professional autonomy concerns have been raised by the mandating of often uniform limited treatment duration for clients who vary in diagnosis, problem severity, and personal resources.

Several issues are relevant to client selection for brief therapy: (a) actual client attendance patterns; (b) empirical studies of determinants of differential outcome for brief and longer therapy; (c) recommendations by brief therapy authors; and (d) the emotional response of psychotherapists to this issue, often derived from political, theoretical, and economic considerations. Each issue will be addressed in this chapter. Certain ethical and humanitarian issues relevant to these issues will also be considered.

PROFESSIONALS' ATTITUDES TOWARD CLIENT SELECTION

While many psychotherapists have an objective and dispassionate approach to client selection for brief therapy, this is a volatile topic for many others, especially those who have had treatment abbreviation forced on them (by insurers' reimbursement policies, etc.). In my graduate training and workshop presentations, I find that many clinicians approach the selection topic by vigorously identifying for whom brief therapy is *not* appropriate, often advocating longer treatment for several client subgroups. The latter has included virtually all diagnoses and problems, with the possible exception of the mildest adjustment disorders. I see this partly as an expression of therapists fighting to retain some of their fading autonomy over treatment (duration) decisions. Consistent with the rationale presented in Chapter Two, this chapter begins with the factual premise that *most clients*, regardless of diagnosis, therapist preference, or insurance plan, *attend treatment only briefly*. For them, the relative impact of brief and longer treatment is a moot point–they *only* attend a brief course of treatment. The issue of selection then must consider which clients can benefit *at all* from brief treatment rather than just debate which clients benefit more from longer than brief therapy. All clients who attend treatment briefly have a right to the most help that can be delivered in that brief time.

This chapter concedes that brief treatment is often selected by the client, not the therapist, thus reducing the importance of the selection issue. The assumption underlying most discussions of client selection for brief therapy is that therapists would have nearly total control of treatment duration if it were not for managed care policies. The data on actual treatment duration previous to managed care's impact, presented in Chapter Two, shows that assumption to be false. Given that clients often select their treatment durations, one of the most important "selection" issues is the identification of those clients who will prefer and are likely to attend only brief treatment. This is addressed at length in the section on negotiating treatment goals and duration in Chapter Seven. Client preferences do not eliminate the therapist's role in client selection, however. Humanitarian, ethical, and cost considerations dictate that we know as much as possible about the probability of treatment success for all treatments regardless of clients' attendance patterns and preferences. One of a therapist's responsibilities is to inform clients about the outcome likely for different treatment durations. Expert recommendations and research findings relevant to which clients and problems are most suited to brief therapy are considered next.

COMMON SELECTION AND EXCLUSION RECOMMENDATIONS

Most brief therapy authors provide (often elaborate) selection criteria, citing client characteristics they claim to be predictive of brief therapy success. Koss and Shiang (1994) and Marmor (1979) have reviewed authors' recommendations and identified several common ones. Both reviews cited good rapport with the therapist, high motivation, focal problems of acute onset, and satisfactory pretreatment or general adjustment as selection criteria. Koss and Shiang (1994) also outlined client characteristics that authors claim exclude them from successful brief therapy, including high anxiety, masochism, negativism, rigidity, self-centeredness, dependency, acting out behaviors, self-destructiveness, passive-dependence, low education, psychosis, organicity, and mental deficiency—a long list of client problems.

These selection and exclusion criteria suffer from two major limitations: first, few of these recommendations have been tested empirically; and second, selection/exclusion criteria are useful only if they are *more* predictive of brief therapy than standard therapy outcome. Reviewing the criteria listed above, it seems likely that they would predict therapy outcome in general rather than differentially predict outcome for brief and standard therapy, a point thoroughly discussed by Bloom (1992). In any case, the utility of these recommendations rests on empirical support for them.

RESEARCH FINDINGS

The key research issue is this: which client characteristics predict superior outcome for longer treatment when compared with brief treatment? (Recall that this question occurs in the context of there being little *overall* differential impact for treatments of varying durations.) Bloom's (1992), Koss and Butcher's (1986), and Koss and Shiang's (1994) reviews of this topic failed to identify any client diagnostic or demographic characteristic to be consistently related to superior outcome for longer treatment. Moreover, Koss and Butcher (1986) concluded that none of the client characteristics that have been studied were any more related to brief than longer therapy outcome. Those client variables included acute problem onset, good previous adjustment, ability to relate, a focal problem, high motivation, and social class.

While Koss and Shiang's (1994) review identified a number of client, therapist, and interactional variables that influence brief therapy outcome, such findings do not aid the decision to use brief or longer treatment with a particular client. What is critical (and absent) is the identification of those variables that predict *different* outcomes for brief and longer-term therapy when clients are randomly assigned to the two.

Despite the lack of supportive research, it *seems* that some clients should benefit more from longer treatment. That is certainly a strong impression of many practitioners. One reason for the lack of findings in this area may be that pursuit of this issue has not been a high research priority—very few studies have set out to identify differential outcome for client subgroups assigned to treatments of varying durations. This reflects the mental health professions' formal opposition to acknowledging that diagnosis (i.e., use of "drgs") might be an appropriate variable for the selection of treatment duration or intensity (Cummings, 1995; Kiesler & Morton, 1988). A second reason for the lack of findings may be that the wrong client variables have been investigated: simple demographics and diagnosis, the most easily investigated of client variables, may be less related to duration-outcome interactions than more complex variables. Client motivational and dispositional variables and client-therapist interaction variables may well better identify the best candidates for treatments of varying durations. This is the case for the prediction of outcome (Beutler, Machado, & Neufeldt, 1994; Garfield, 1994) and continuance (Pekarik, 1985, 1991a; Wierzbicki & Pekarik, 1993) in general.

Two reports, taken together, do offer clues to a rational way to select clients for brief and longer treatment. Shapiro et al. (1994), like others, found that there was little *overall* outcome difference between shorter (eight sessions) and longer (16 sessions) treatment for depressed clients. But the most severely disturbed clients (a minority of those treated) benefited more from the longer treatment, and the less severely disturbed benefited as much from the briefer treatment. The superiority of longer treatment for the severely disturbed was transient; there were no outcome differences between briefer and longer treatments at one-year follow-up (Shapiro et al., 1995). Miller and Hester (1986) summarized comparisons of alcohol treatments of varying intensity (outpatient vs. inpatient) rather than duration. Like Shapiro et al., 1994, they reported no overall outcome differences but noted that the more socially disorganized (transient, unemployed) clients benefited more from intensive treatment, while the more socially integrated majority did better with less intensive treatment. It is important to note that in both studies the most problematic *minority* benefited incrementally from longer or more intensive treatment while the *majority* benefited as much or more from briefer or less intensive treatment. It should also be noted that the Shapiro et al. (1994) study was of brief (16 sessions) vs. very brief (eight sessions) treatment. In conclusion, these two studies suggest that more problematic clients (with greater symptom severity and fewer resources) may benefit from longer treatment while the average and better functioning clients (the majority) may benefit as much or even more from briefer treatment. (Unfortunately, more disturbed clients are *not* more likely to actually *participate* in treatment for a longer time than less disturbed clients.) This admittedly speculative analysis suggests some tentative recommendations: use briefer therapy with moderately disturbed clients and longer (though not necessarily long-term) therapy with those who have severe symptoms and fewer resources. Obviously, more research that addresses benefit of treatments of varying durations for different client subgroups is greatly needed.

ETHICS AND TREATMENT SELECTION

In order to address ethical issues associated with brief psychotherapy, it is important to distinguish brief psychotherapy from the service delivery arrangements (i.e., managed care) where it is often conducted. As others have noted, there is a host of ethical issues associated with managed care (Haas & Cummings, 1991; Newman & Bricklin, 1991), primarily concerned with denial of care to those in need. But brief therapy per se, especially when delivered as a treatment chosen by the client and with access to longer care if desired and needed, probably poses no more (though perhaps somewhat different) ethical risks than standard psychotherapy. Given the compatibility of brief therapy with most clients' treatment preferences, brief therapy may even possess certain ethical safeguards that standard therapy does not. These mainly have to do with maintaining client treatment choices.

Medical ethicists have dealt extensively with the relative power that the client and health care provider should exert in treatment choice. Their conclusions are clear and unambiguous: the patient has final authority in such matters, even when in opposition to the physician's counsel. The problem of undue influence by the physician due to status and authority has been addressed explicitly: "Although *patients have the legal and moral authority over physician-patient relationships*, physicians have enormous power in these relationships. They can shape the course and moral dimensions of medical care by their psychological dominance, specialized knowledge, and technical skills. *The physician's power can . . . destroy the fragile moral autonomy of the patient*" (Jonson, Siegler, & Winslade, 1986, pg. 49, italics added). In psychotherapy, unequivocal statements about the legitimacy of client choices are difficult to find, and some authors have acknowledged this as a problem (Keith-Spiegel & Koocher, 1985). The history of psychotherapists' viewing client opposition to treatment as a "resistance" to overcome has probably contributed to the psychotherapy field's neglect of client rights in choosing treatments.

In medical as well as mental health settings there are occasions when the helping professional recommends a treatment that is different from the client's preference. Even when this occurs *with an emotionally upset client*, it is regarded as *unethical* for a professional to pursue a course of treatment at variance with the client's choice (Jonson, Siegler, & Winslade, 1986). In brief therapy, the characteristic frank, open discussion of treatment goals between client and therapist and the acknowledgment of the legitimacy of modest goals chosen by clients are clearly compatible with the ethical principles described above. This avoids the ethical problem of too vigorously trying to overcome client resistance at the price of eroding the "fragile moral autonomy" of clients.

There is the prospect in standard therapy of the therapist encouraging longer treatment than desired by the client; certainly there are powerful fiscal and convenience incentives for doing so (Budman & Gurman, 1983, 1988; Haas & Cummings, 1991). The huge disparity between therapist preferences/prescription and client preferences/actual treatment duration further suggest there is a risk here of therapists' exerting inordinate influence regarding treatment duration and goals. The kinds of brief therapy procedures outlined in Chapter Seven's description of goal-setting, with its great sensitivity to client treatment preferences, seems a good way to avoid this ethical risk.

There are, of course, some special ethical issues associated with treatment abbreviation. A brief therapist may run the risk of implying that adequate help can be delivered in too brief a treatment, might ignore the possibility of success with long-term treatment, or might neglect to treat important problems outside of the selected treatment focus. These are legitimate concerns but there are clear procedures for greatly minimizing their risk. As recommended and elaborated in Chapters Five through Ten, continual assessment throughout the course of treatment, review of goals and problems at initially agreed upon termination, access to continued treatment beyond the initially agreed upon treatment duration, and other safeguards can minimize most special brief therapy risks.

CONCLUSIONS AND RECOMMENDATIONS

Given the outcome data, actual attendance patterns, client preferences, and ethical issues considered in this chapter, it is not surprising that many brief therapy authors advocate that a brief course of treatment be used initially with virtually all outpatients, to be followed by longer treatment only if the client wants it and has not benefited adequately from brief therapy (Bloom, 1992; Budman & Gurman, 1988; Hoffman & Remmel, 1975; Wolberg, 1980). As the evidence presented shows, this is a very defensible position, especially for clients with moderate to mild problems. A strictly empirical approach to treatment duration would dictate brief treatment for almost all cases, given the lack of consistent evidence for the superiority of longer treatments in general or for client subgroups.

But there are good arguments for the selective use of longer-term treatment. First, there is the empirical support for long*er* (if not long) therapy for those with very severe problems or social disorganization, as implied by the Miller & Hester (1986) and Shapiro et al. (1994) reports. In addition, there is strong reason to believe that the research has not adequately addressed this issue.

Within a brief therapy model, there are some guidelines for longer-term therapy assignment. Clients who have multiple areas of dysfunction and wish to work on them would certainly be appropriate for long*er* treatment. There may be specific disorders or client subgroups who require a minimum treatment duration for any benefit or who improve more with longer treatment. Research using random assignment of client subgroups to treatments of varying durations is the (methodologically) ideal way to explore this. Unfortunately, there is little research of this sort currently being done, and the difficulties in doing it make its wide-scale application unlikely.

Research Recommendations

There is a much easier research alternative to investigating these duration-outcome issues that can be done at almost any clinic setting—the conduct of post hoc *dose-effect* studies for client subgroups. I caution the reader that I use the term *dose-effect* with reservation in the discussion that follows. True dose-effect studies require an experimental design: random assignment of cases to treatments of varying dosage (that is, sessions, in the case of psychotherapy research). Here I describe a correlational analogue of dose-effect—a study of outcome for clients who have attended varying numbers of sessions but whose treatment duration is self-selected rather than experimentally controlled. I use the term dose-effect only because it is commonly (mis)used in the research literature to describe this type of passive-observational research. All that is needed for this research are client outcome measures at three or more time points and client characteristic information. (See Howard et al., 1986, 1993; and Kopta et al., 1994 for more detailed descriptions.) Essentially, the investigator simply identifies problem change at various time points, noting if greater improvement occurs over increased sessions. This method cannot prove that more treatment causes greater improvement in the cases where duration is associated with improvement, because this is a type of passive-observer (or correlational) researcher. A lack of improvement with increased sessions for client subgroups *does* suggest that longer treatment may be unwarranted for those subgroups, however. A logical (and conservative) strategy would be to (a) do much more passive-observer dose-effect research; (b) based on such studies, identify client groups who do and do not benefit from increased therapy duration; (c) consider longer treatment for client groups who benefit from increased treatment and brief treatment for those who do not; and then (d) follow-up these interim studies with true experimental studies (using random assignment of the client groups to treatments of varying durations). In addition to the usual criteria for good applied research, there are two keys to the successful conduct of "analogue" dose-effect research: first, the inclusion of both client and therapist outcome measures (therapist measures are quite biased in favor of longer treatment); and second, the reliable identification of important client characteristics (including diagnostic, motivational, and other variables) that might be associated with differential outcome for treatments of varying durations. There are also a number of methodological refinements that can create quasi-experiments from this essentially correlational approach, thereby improving confidence that treatment sessions and outcome relationships might be deterministic. The reader is referred to Howard et al. (1986); Howard et al. (1993); and Stiles and Shapiro (1994) for discussion of relevant issues.

Summary

In summary, more research needs to be done before we can specify the ideal treatment duration for different client groups. But this issue is often moot, since most clients attend treatment briefly regardless of therapist recommendations. The proper therapist role then becomes to describe to clients the likely outcomes attainable by treatments of varying durations (techniques for doing this are described in detail in Chapter Seven). At present there is not adequate empirical research to provide clear guidelines for this, however. A combination of the therapist's own caseload observations along with the duration-outcome research such as cited in Chapter Two probably provide the best guidelines at present. Hopefully, more research such as that reported by Shapiro et al. (1994, 1995) and Miller and Hester (1986) will become available in the future, further assisting client selection and prediction of outcomes for varying treatment durations.

The issues reviewed in this chapter suggest that brief therapy can be considered for a very wide range of clients. It is appropriate for most clients with mild to moderate problems and even those with more severe problems, especially if the latter are unwilling to attend longer treatment, as commonly occurs.

Chapter Four

A Model for Conceptualizing the Treatment Abbreviation Process

Most approaches to doing brief therapy are not simple adaptations of a long-term therapy to a briefer format. Quite the contrary—although many have a theoretical allegiance with one of the standard therapies, most are complex undertakings that provide a unique theory of psychopathology and therapeutic change processes along with a novel set of associated treatment techniques, all of which are conducive to brief treatment. In the process, most also rely on general abbreviating strategies that are independent of any particular theoretical orientation or treatment technique, such as maintenance of a narrow treatment focus and pursuit of modest treatment goals. Because these latter general abbreviating strategies are coordinated with a particular author's theory and technique, they are often not conceived nor portrayed as general strategies; they are expressed in the idiosyncratic language of a particular approach. It is only after reviewing a number of different approaches to brief therapy that one can identify that some abbreviating strategies are common even though they are often portrayed in differing theoretical language.

It is this book's thesis that the general abbreviating strategies alone are sufficient for treatment abbreviation if they are described in sufficient and jargon-free detail. This has the great advantage of allowing psychotherapists to simply adapt their current theory, style, and techniques to a brief treatment format. It is the goal of this book to help therapists accomplish that. The theory behind this book, then, is not a general theory of psychopathology or therapy change, but a theory about what contributes to treatment abbreviation and effective brief interventions.

I believe that certain core abbreviating strategies common to most brief therapies are necessary and sufficient for treatment abbreviation (if pursued in the context of acceptance of brief therapy's desirability for at least some clients). Most important are four interrelated components: (1) rapid assessment and case conceptualization; (2) establishment of a narrow treatment focus; (3) negotiation of modest but meaningful treatment goals; and (4) the adaptation of traditional treatment techniques to a brief format. Means of achieving each of these four strategies will be described later in the text and create the technique portion of the book. These characteristics, gathered from my own review of brief therapies and a review of several reviews of brief therapy (Bloom, 1992; Budman & Gurman, 1988; Koss & Butcher, 1986; Koss & Shiang, 1994; Pekarik, 1990) are each frequently cited by brief therapy proponents.

CONTRIBUTIONS OF "COMMON CHARACTERISTICS" TO TREATMENT ABBREVIATION

The four key components of treatment abbreviation derive from and incorporate the longer list of common characteristics of brief therapies introduced in Chapter One. The contribution of each characteristic from that longer list is presented below, along with citation of the chapters in this book where each is further addressed.

Limited but Flexible Use of Time

The recommended treatment duration for brief therapy varies widely across approaches. As Budman and Gurman (1983, 1988) suggest, the key may be time sensitivity–trying to deliver the most effective treatment within the shortest time–rather than any particular session limitation. But time limitation per se can have a powerful effect: much of the research comparing the impact of time-limited and time-unlimited treatment (which generally finds equal impact) includes treatment simply abbreviated by time, without training in brief therapy technique.

Time limitations or self-imposed time sensitivity accomplish several things. They (a) motivate client and therapist to begin treatment and problem-solving from the first session; (b) promote optimism and expectation of treatment benefit through the therapist's confidence that improvement is possible in a short time; (c) imply a frame for the scope of treatment—that it will be oriented to specific problems rather than general personality (or lifestyle) reconstruction, and (d) communicate that client and therapist must work hard and stay on task throughout treatment in order to achieve benefit.

Rather than routinely employ a weekly 50-minute hour, the brief therapist uses time as it suits the therapy tasks. Hence, the need for time flexibility. Fifteen-minute sessions may be adequate to monitor ongoing successful implementation of a treatment strategy, while two consecutive hours in a crisis may be more valuable than several more hours delivered at the rate of one hour per week. The issues of time and efficiency are interwoven throughout this book rather than covered in a discrete chapter.

A Clear, Specific Treatment Focus

This is the hallmark of brief therapy. A clear, usually single and narrow, focus is most often cited as the most important characteristic of brief therapy. Adherence to such a focus is what allows treatment to be brief: brief treatment aimed at broad or multiple issues would probably be doomed to failure. By concentrating efforts on a single, narrow focus, there is a great chance of impacting on that focus. This increases treatment impact, efficiency, and the client's and therapist's expectation of benefit. Although psychotherapists are traditionally trained to be broad in their focus, clients typically want treatment to address a single focus (see Chapter Two).

As one of the core common elements, the importance and implications of a narrow focus are elaborated in Chapter Six, along with a description of strategies for identifying and maintaining a narrow focus.

Limited Treatment Goals

By limiting treatment goals within the chosen focal issue, the scope and duration of treatment are further limited. Limiting goals to modest, achievable ones accomplishes many of the same things as a narrow focus. Being achievable and within grasp, clients typically have high expectations for the attainment of modest goals and work hard to obtain them.

A very important aspect of brief therapy goal selection is that it is done largely by the client. While focus identification requires client input, the therapist's specialized knowledge and objectivity often gives him/her greater influence in establishing a focus. This is not so with goal selection: the client's view takes precedence over the therapist's. The therapist's job is to identify a range of goals and estimate the effort and time required to attain them. This makes a key contribution to the "consumer-friendliness" of brief therapy and may contribute to its lower dropout rate. It is primarily for this reason that the negotiation of goals is one of the core common elements of brief therapy, and elaborated in Chapter Seven.

Focus on Present Stress

Clients typically enter psychotherapy because of the presence of a stressor with which they are unable to cope. Even though therapists may view a problem as rooted in theory-based determinants such as illogical beliefs, conditioned responses, or unconscious motives, brief therapists keep a clear connection between these less salient (to the client) notions and the client's concerns in order to maintain client motivation. Focusing on current stressors can also help the brief therapist identify an appropriate brief therapy focal issue: current stressors are usually more appropriate foci than broader issues that contribute to them. This issue is primarily addressed in the chapter on focus identification (Chapter Six).

Rapid Assessment

With time at a premium, assessment must be rapid in order to allocate adequate time for intervention. The major abbreviating strategy is to primarily assess the focal problem rather than all areas of functioning (or personality) of the client. Assessment and focus identification are therefore highly interrelated.

Many therapists are concerned that rapid assessment will be superficial or fail to identify critical information, especially regarding (a) the risk of harm to self or others and (b) a diagnosis that might have treatment or prognostic implications. These are legitimate concerns and warrant elaborate consideration. Rapid assessment is considered one of the core abbreviation characteristics; strategies for abbreviating assessment and dealing with common therapist concerns about rapid assessment are described in Chapter Five.

High Level of Client and Therapist Activity

The brief therapist "fills" every session of brief therapy in order to get the most out of it. This does not mean the brief therapist rushes therapy or overburdens the client, but that s/he is optimally active. The brief therapist accomplishes this by structuring sessions to address the focus and by pursuing an objective clearly linked to the focus and goals each session. This often entails that the therapist is direct, and actively formulates and implements interventions for use both in and outside of sessions. It may involve advising the client to engage in activities but it can also involve purposeful experiential interventions by the therapist, such as timely provision of empathy, warmth, and support.

Similarly, clients are typically required to do "homework," link up with community and personal resources, and otherwise engage in therapeutic activity in and outside of the sessions. Client and therapist activity are addressed in the chapters on goal establishment (Chapter Seven) and treatment implementation (Chapter Eight), where special attention is paid to the importance of creating goals for each session as a means of maintaining high activity levels.

Use of Eclectic Therapy Techniques

A theme throughout this book is that brief therapists must be pragmatic, using whatever techniques work most efficiently, even when they are derived from a theoretical orientation other than their own. This is compatible with current proposals that empirically "proven" techniques be identified and employed by all therapists. Such proposals are increasingly being made by both professional mental health associations and health care provider organizations (Chambless, 1993). Ways of adapting such techniques to one's preferred style (and translating them into the language and concepts of one's preferred theory) are described in Chapter Eight.

THE FOUR KEY ELEMENTS OF TREATMENT ABBREVIATION

All the foregoing common characteristics of treatment abbreviation are probably important, as may be some others not listed but cited by various authors. Many of the common characteristics overlap with each other or are subsumed by others, however. In this book, it was easy and convenient to: include "focusing on present stress" under the broader topic of establishing a clear, specific focus; address "high levels of client and therapist activity" in the chapters on goal-setting and treatment implementation; and describe eclectic techniques in the treatment implementation chapter.

Each of what are referred to as the four key elements (rapid assessment, identification of a narrow focus, negotiation of modest goals, and adaptation of traditional techniques) has an especially important relationship to treatment abbreviation. None of the four is easily subsumed by the others: each is fundamental. Each is acknowledged as a common element in treatment abbreviation by most brief therapy reviewers (Bloom, 1992; Budman & Gurman, 1983, 1988; Koss & Butcher, 1986; Koss & Shiang, 1994). Rapid assessment, focus identification, and goal negotiation are interrelated activities that typically occur in the first or second session of brief therapy. Together, they orient the client and therapist to the pace and scope of treatment. Once they are accomplished, brief treatment follows naturally, logically, and almost (but not quite) inevitably. Operationally, they are so interwoven that it is often impossible to identify isolated segments of therapy that deal exclusively with one alone. They are separated in this discussion as a matter of convenience, to allow a simplified description of what often occurs simultaneously.

There are some additional reasons that the four key elements have been selected for elaboration. Rapid assessment often requires consideration because it elicits concerns about legal and ethical issues: what if important information is overlooked in an effort to abbreviate assessment? In addition, certain assessment practices (e.g., the routine use of psychological tests or creation of elaborate genograms) may be sometimes incompatible with brief therapy, so revision of some standard assessment practices may be necessary. More generally, assessment is traditionally identified as separate from treatment, so this text follows traditional form by devoting a separate chapter to assessment (it also shows how to change that tradition by intervening in the first session of brief therapy).

The importance of focusing in brief therapy cannot be overstated. Most standard therapy approaches advise against the narrow focusing done in brief therapy. As described in Chapter Two, even orientations that are self-consciously narrow in their treatment focus are typically too broad for brief therapy; like U. S. foreign troop deployments, therapists often suffer from "mission-creep," a gradual task expansion beyond those originally identified in order to deal with additional problems.

Some aspects of traditional training are also incompatible with the way goals are negotiated in brief therapy. The broad notion of "resistance," employed by virtually all orientations in some form, often creates a distrust of client-identified goals by conceptualizing client treatment choices as an outgrowth of their emotional problems–clients cannot be trusted to choose what is best for them. This is especially true when modest goals are chosen. In brief therapy, clients are often encouraged to make informed choices about goals and granted the credibility to make them.

All of these first three elements, then, are not only critical to the performance of brief therapy, but standard training is often incompatible with their implementation. This makes it important to have some structured training in these skills as provided in Chapters Five, Six, and Seven. The fourth element, *adaptation of standard techniques* to a brief format, is different from the first three. We might think of brief therapy as being condensed into two basic factors, one concerned with treatment target selection (addressed by the first three elements) and the second concerned with intervention (addressed by the fourth element). In my training with practitioners and graduate students, I have found that adaptation of standard techniques follows quite easily for clinicians once the first three elements have been successfully addressed. All that is needed at that point are a general strategy for applying techniques in a brief format, a few specific guidelines, some case examples, and encouragement to use their intervention skills in a brief format. That is what is provided in Chapter Eight.

PHILOSOPHY, VALUES, AND ATTITUDES

The strategies and skills described in this book are unlikely to be executed competently unless the therapist believes that brief treatment can be a very good thing for clients. Research suggests that therapists' attitudes about brief therapy are important. Burlingame et al. (1989) found that experienced therapists were not deficient in skills needed to do brief treatment, but required increased acceptance of it in order to be effective–brief therapy effectiveness increased as therapist attitudes changed during a brief therapy training program. My own training program (Pekarik, 1994), which had the effect of increasing treatment satisfaction for clients of trainees, devoted half of training to rationale and therapist attitude change. And, finally, Bolter, Levenson, & Alvarez (1990) found that attitudes (regarding potential for significant client improvement over a short time) distinguished brief and long-term therapists.

The use of the brief treatment strategies described in this book make most sense within a context of certain attitudes about therapy; they are the integrating factors that pull together the common elements of brief therapy. These attitudes are shared by most clients: they are compatible with clients' preferences for treatment to be efficient and problem-oriented.

A word of caution is in order before addressing attitude further: most readers have been oriented in their training and "therapy culture" toward attitudes incompatible with those of brief therapy. One of the goals of this book is to change attitudes. It is hoped that these first four chapters (especially Chapter Two) will contribute to that change, and that the technique chapters (five through eight) will make a further contribution. But the ultimate attitude change is associated with doing planned brief therapy on a fairly wide scale and seeing its successful impact.

Several authors have dealt extensively with the therapist values associated with brief therapy (Bloom, 1984; Budman & Gurman, 1983; Koss & Shiang, 1994). The key attitude seems to be fairly simple: rather than idealize the long-term intensive treatment pursued and wanted by only a small minority of clients, the brief therapist enthusiastically and optimistically pursues the same cost-effective goals desired by clients; s/he celebrates the prospect of delivering efficient treatment of the same scope envisioned by clients.

The brief therapist is not frustrated by a client's lack of motivation to pursue numerous goals or personality change; buoyed by research that shows that brief therapy has a record of delivering an excellent outcome and cost-benefit ratio, s/he regards clients' modest goals as legitimate and sensible. These attitudes address the purpose and proposed scope of therapy.

The brief therapist is both more and less optimistic about therapy than his/her long-term counterpart: more optimistic about the range of clients and problems treatable, more optimistic about the probability of achieving modest goals, more optimistic about the (short) time required to help clients, but less optimistic about the prospects of personality change and inoculation against future mental health problems (the notion of a "cure"). All the brief therapist attitudes described here are compatible with the psychotherapy research findings described in Chapter Two. Consistent with that empirical framework, the brief therapist acknowledges a place for long-term therapy suggested by the few reports that suggest its superior outcome for certain client subgroups (see Chapters Two and Three). This is tempered, however, by the facts that (a) most who could benefit from longer treatment will terminate early in treatment and can get some benefit from the shorter treatment; and (b) more research needs to be done in order to document the incremental value of longer treatment for client subgroups, since the overwhelming evidence supports superior efficiency and cost-benefit for brief therapy across aggregated client samples.

Chapter Five

Rapid Assessment and Case Conceptualization

The tasks involved in selecting a treatment issue–assessment, problem conceptualization, focus identification, and goal negotiation–are highly interrelated. It is virtually impossible to do any one of these in isolation: much of assessment addresses the emerging focus; problem conceptualization affects what is selected as a focus; and assessment information is relied on to create a problem conceptualization. This should be kept in mind as each part is treated (somewhat artificially, for ease of discussion) individually in this and subsequent chapters.

CASE CONCEPTUALIZATION

Case conceptualization refers to the way that a therapist understands the nature of a client's problems. This requires an understanding of the specific aspects of a client's particular situation, and so is dependent on the details provided by assessment inquiries. But an important aspect of case conceptualization is present before the initial assessment–one's theoretical orientation, which encompasses theories of personality/psychopathology and therapeutic change. This text's approach assumes that most clinicians already have a theoretical orientation that works well for them–that is the case for most practitioners. For students, coursework on theories usually provides an adequate theoretical background for the conduct of psychotherapy. A special theory of personality/psychopathology is not needed in order to do brief therapy, though a theory of some kind is important. A theoretical orientation is important in brief therapy for the same reasons it is in longer therapy; it:

- guides assessment by providing theory-linked issues to investigate (e.g., early childhood experience, illogical beliefs)
- helps the therapist understand the causes of the client's problems
- gives the therapist a way to help the client understand the nature and cause of the problem
- provides treatment strategies and techniques

As noted throughout this book, brief therapies have been derived from all the major contemporary theoretical orientations, and a wide range of them have been demonstrated as effective. Almost any orientation can be compatible with brief therapy as long as there is an acknowledgment that child and adult adjustment is a continuous process with opportunities for change of established patterns and acquisition of new skills throughout life. This entails an emphasis on current life functioning although it acknowledges that early experience can impact on current adjustment.

As with traditional therapy, the locus of change identified by a theory can vary in brief therapy. That locus might be overt behavior, inner experience, internal defenses, or any number of other theory-linked phenomena. For those who are skeptical about the prospects of adapting their orientation to a brief format, I refer you to the brief therapy text "anthologies" that have chapters written by experts from many different orientations (Wells & Giannetti, 1990 and Zeig & Gilligan, 1990 are good examples).

Case Conceptualization Elements Common to All Brief Therapies

While brief therapies associated with different theoretical orientations vary in their frameworks for understanding behavior, they all share certain ideas about the *scope* of therapy change. This aspect of case conceptualization is common to virtually all brief therapy approaches. The common conceptualization element consists of (a) acknowledging the utility of *narrow* treatment foci and *modest* goals, (b) strategies for identifying such foci and goals, and (c) ways of applying treatment techniques to such foci and goals.

Therapists who learn to do brief therapy typically develop a view of clients, problems, and therapy that is significantly affected by the philosophy and strategies associated with treatment abbreviation. That view follows from learning why and how to abbreviate treatment, and will be fully in place after brief therapy training is complete. At this stage, it is sufficient to have been acquainted with brief therapy's rationale and the overview of abbreviating strategies that has been provided thus far. The sum total of the contents of this book provides the means for altering one's view and practice of psychotherapy and, thus, can contribute to case conceptualization by providing an alternative treatment process rather than a general theory of personality/psychopathology.

RAPID ASSESSMENT

There are three basic components to brief therapy assessment:

1. Gathering information on current and past functioning relevant to the client's current plight.
2. Use of this information in order to understand the cause of the client's current problems, i.e., a theoretical conceptualization of the problem.
3. Identifying a treatment focus and gathering enough information about it to formulate a treatment plan.

These components are similar to the process of assessment in standard therapy. A major difference is that at least a preliminary assessment is completed by the end of the first session so that an active intervention can begin at that time. The major abbreviating strategy is to rather quickly narrow the assessment to particular adjustment problems rather than general functioning or personality. Generally, this means that assessment is restricted to the presenting problem and directly relevant information.

Bloom (1992, pg. 105) has succinctly described this strategy in the context of his radical single-session therapy: "I avoid collecting demographic information or doing a traditional mental status examination. It is my experience that . . . the most important information will emerge in the normal course of the interview." He also cautions against digressions into tangential topics ". . . I find myself wishing I could explore some little phrase for just a few minutes, but such diversions have nearly always turned out to be errors . . . not only is there no time to explore side issues, but . . . such exploration detracts from the potential effectiveness of therapy" (Bloom, 1992, pg. 106).

By beginning the first session with such common problem-orienting questions as "What kind of concerns brought you here to the clinic?" "How can I be of help to you?" or "Tell me about the concerns that prompted you to make an appointment with me," the therapist can begin an appropriate brief therapy assessment. Generally, the brief therapist encourages the client to tell his or her story about the problems. As more information is divulged, the brief therapist must identify potential foci, then increasingly address these as more information increases the therapist's confidence in these topics as worthy foci. A thorough and detailed assessment of the selected focus usually occurs in brief therapy. But the focus is a relatively small part of the client's overall experience, even though it can have pervasive effect on adjustment. By concentrating on fairly narrow realms of inquiry, assessment is greatly abbreviated. Assessment, then, is abbreviated by first, orienting toward clients' presenting problems and closely related information, and second, gradually narrowing the scope of inquiry to a single or very few potential foci. Clearly, facility in selecting a focus is a major step in assessment abbreviation, and will be thoroughly explored in Chapter Six.

A major difference between traditional and brief assessment is that, in brief assessment, the therapist does not necessarily thoroughly assess every aspect of all life problems. If there is a problem area that the client is not particularly concerned about, the brief therapist may only assess it enough to confirm that it is indeed not severe nor a client priority. This, more than anything, abbreviates assessment.

Prerequisite Skills and Potential Risks in Assessment Abbreviation

Premature narrowing of assessment information runs the risk of excluding important information about a client's potential harm to self or others, or diagnosis of incipient signs of a severe disorder. Brief therapy assessors have the same legal and ethical obligations to make accurate assessments in these areas as all mental health professionals; the conduct of brief therapy is never a justification for an inadequate assessment. Given the brief therapist's restricted assessment time, this means that brief therapists must be especially good at assessment. In particular, brief therapists must be aware of the risk factors associated with suicide (Shneidman, 1985) and aggression (Monahan, 1984) potential. In addition, the brief therapist should be a very competent diagnostician so that signs of substance abuse and severe disorders, or even prodromal predictors of severe disorders, are readily recognized. Competence in these areas should be mastered before attempting unsupervised brief therapy with general caseloads.

When indicators of severe or life-threatening conditions are present, assessment and treatment of such conditions automatically becomes the brief therapy focus. Even when other, normally appropriate foci, are present, they are secondary to the aforementioned conditions. Similarly, a client's substance abuse typically interferes with addressing other foci, and needs to be accurately diagnosed and given initial treatment priority (recall the excellent track record of brief therapy for substance abuse cited in Chapter Two).

ASSESSMENT MODELS

The general principles outlined above can be adapted to almost any general approach to psychotherapy. As long as those general principles are followed, no particular assessment model is required for assessment abbreviation. Nevertheless, certain assessment models are especially well-suited to an abbreviated format. Two assessment models derived from very different theoretical orientations are presented below in order to (a) provide readers with a diversity of brief assessment strategies that they can adopt wholly or partly and (b) demonstrate that radically different treatment orientations can indeed be used in brief therapy.

Budman and Gurman's Interpersonal-Developmental-Existential Model

Budman and Gurman (1988) posit that interpersonal, developmental, and existential issues are common reasons that clients seek psychotherapeutic help. They acknowledge that their approach has intrapsychic, existential, human potential, and interpersonal theoretical elements. Given their emphasis on adult development, their approach also appears compatible with neo-analytic theorizing such as Erik Erikson's (1959).

They identify what they claim are the five most common foci presented in brief therapy and use them to provide a "decision tree" for prioritizing focus selection. Relying on their five foci can greatly abbreviate the assessment process because awareness of these as high probability problems provides the therapist with potential assessment and treatment targets once their presence is verified as a client concern. The five common foci are:

1. losses
2. developmental dysynchronies, which occur when age or stage of life-related achievements and expectations are not met
3. interpersonal conflicts
4. symptomatic presentations, which are described as discrete dysfunctional symptoms such as "habit disorders, sexual dysfunctions, fears, and phobias."
5. personality disorders

Budman and Gurman (1988) indicate that loss, developmental dysynchrony, or interpersonal conflict are most likely to be identified as the client's reason for seeking treatment. If none are, then symptomatic focus is the next most plausible focus. If none of the four can be successfully targeted and character issues are present, then personality disorder is an appropriate, but longer, treatment focus.

The authors contend that asking why a client elects to seek treatment at the particular time chosen will help the brief therapist identify the developmental-existential aspects of a client's problems. They therefore recommend asking "Why now?" as a critical initial step in brief assessment. They also recommend that the brief therapist consider a number of other assessment questions related to their approach. These questions primarily address the client's developmental stage, anniversaries of important events, social support, external pressure to enter treatment, and substance abuse.

Budman and Gurman's (1988) approach illustrates the close relationship among case conceptualization, assessment, and focusing. The assessment checklist they provide is clearly oriented to identifying one of the common foci, which in turn are derived from their interpersonal-developmental-existential conceptualization base. As this summary illustrates, all three (conceptualization, assessment, and focusing) are integral components of the process of identifying what will be addressed in treatment. Assessment in their approach is abbreviated by often restricting it to a few plausible treatment issues.

Budman and Gurman's (1988) brief therapy assessment strategy would probably be especially appealing to therapists aligned with one of the theoretical orientations from which their approach was derived, especially since they also describe "orientation-compatible" treatments for each of their five common foci. Because they have done a good job of using jargon-free, "generic" psychotherapy language and constructs, their assessment strategy is also suitable as a complement to other assessment approaches.

Behavioral Assessment

Unlike Budman and Gurman's (1988), the behavioral approach to treatment is not necessarily brief. Despite an efficiency often-cited by its advocates, in Chapter Two it was documented why behavioral treatment is not necessarily brief therapy. Nevertheless, many aspects of behavioral assessment are extremely well-suited to rapid assessment. This suitability derives from both theoretical and technical aspects of the behavioral approach to assessment.

The behavioral approach is by nature problem and present-oriented: behavioral theory cites symptoms rather than presumed unobservable determinants as the most appropriate treatment foci. The main modification needed to adapt standard behavioral approaches to a brief format is the narrowing of focus to one or a few problems rather than the usual pursuit of all or general areas of dysfunction. When applied to a narrow focus, behavioral strategies can provide an excellent brief therapy assessment.

Behavioral assessment typically includes asking the client why help was sought at the particular time chosen. This is done because of an assumption that the current environment elicits or inhibits the conduct of adjustment-relevant behavior. Although for somewhat different rationales, then, behavioral assessment and Budman and

Gurman's (1988) assessment both prescribe asking the "Why now?" question.

A comprehensive description of behavioral assessment is beyond the scope of this book. Two important aspects of behavioral assessment that are especially compatible with a brief (and eclectic) approach are illustrated: (1) the construction of problems as behavioral deficits or excesses, and (2) the specification of antecedents and consequences of problem behavior.

Behavioral Excesses and Deficits

One of the most basic aspects of behavioral assessment is the depiction of problems as behaviors engaged in too much (excesses) or too little (deficits) (Gelfand & Hartmann, 1984). The quantity can be defined in terms of frequency, severity, or duration. Implicit in this strategy is the use of the operational definition, that is, describing phenomena in observable and measurable terms. One of the reasons for doing this is that it forces the therapist and client to discourse in terms of directly observable phenomena, the stock-in-trade of behaviorists (though it should be noted that cognitive-behaviorists have adapted this to include excessive and deficient cognitions as well). This can be especially useful when clients describe problems with vague or general terms that communicate very imprecisely. "I'm having a nervous breakdown," "I'm depressed," "I'm having a mid-life crisis," "My spouse is a bastard," "My child drives me crazy" are all common examples of this sort of imprecision. Assessment can be especially difficult when a client describes a problem in terms of misused theoretical concepts or popular psychology notions that communicate imprecisely. Clients who state that they wish to get in contact with their inner child, or are codependent may have any number of different treatment concerns underlying these expressions. Asking clients exactly what they (or someone else) are doing overtly that is problematic can provide a mutually understood vocabulary for discussing problems and identifying foci.

A simulated case example of a client who initially presented his problem as a "mid-life crisis" is described in detail in Chapters Six, Seven, and Eight. When initially asked what he meant by that, the client described a host of vaguely described problems: he had "low self-esteem," "felt like a loser," "couldn't do anything right," was "always out of it," "couldn't get along with anyone," and was "out of control." While it was useful to have this initial problem depiction, more specificity was needed to accurately assess the problem. By asking the client "What do you *do* that makes you feel that you can't get along with anyone?" the client was able to identify arguments with his work supervisor as the primary interpersonal conflict. By further asking about the frequency of these arguments, the client noted that they had about one overt disagreement each week. In this case, the translation of "couldn't get along with anyone" into overt behavior both clarified the nature of the interpersonal problem and was therapeutic: it helped change the client's view of himself as someone who had general interpersonal problems to someone who had weekly conflicts with a single other person. Similar questioning about the other issues yielded other specific symptoms and problems as depicted in Chapter Six.

Specification of Problem Antecedents and Consequences

Behavioral theory contends that problem behaviors are often elicited by particular environmental events, places, or people (through theoretical constructs such as conditioned and discriminative stimuli), and are therefore predictable to a degree. Inquiring about the particular situations in which problems occur has a theoretical rationale, namely, the identification of stimuli that elicit the problems–this presumes a cause and effect relationship that can be used in devising a treatment regimen. The identification of environmental antecedents also helps narrow the definition of the problem. If a client initially describes himself as irritable it might be tempting to ascribe this to a character trait of general irritability–a general problem and a broad treatment issue. But if a particular person in a particular setting elicits most of the irritable behavior, then the treatment issue can be narrowed dramatically to those specific stimuli.

Operant paradigms suggest that much problematic behavior is maintained by its consequences (reward and punishment). In a case example presented later, one of the client's problems is his difficulty completing a master's thesis. Assessment revealed that when he sat down to work on his thesis the client typically became anxious and often achieved immediate anxiety relief by electing to engage in recreational activity with his partner, who was usually available as an eager participant. His work environment rewarded the cessation of work. This discovery pointed toward certain interventions and by itself was therapeutic: it replaced the client's characterological understanding of his procrastination with a much narrower construction of the problem. Instead of being lazy, incompetent, or procrastinating (all broad treatment issues), the focus narrowed to reducing the anxiety and eliminating work escape options, two far narrower treatment targets.

Budman and Gurman's (1988) strategies and behavioral assessment strategies derive from very different theoretical orientations and approaches to treatment, yet both are very compatible with brief assessment. The two approaches achieve abbreviation in different ways. Budman and Gurman do so by creating a short list of high probability potential foci, each of which is fairly tightly conceptualized and appropriate for brief therapy. In brief behavioral assessment, abbreviation is a two step process. First, the assessment is intrinsically brief because it is problem- and present-oriented rather than personality oriented. But this is not sufficient for brief therapy—often this brief assessment is applied to a large number of different problems for a given client, turning it into quite a long assessment. The behaviorist must limit the treatment focus to an issue or two in order to accomplish a brief assessment and treatment. Procedures for narrowing the focus, such as those covered in the next chapter, are often needed to make behavioral assessment brief.

The purpose of presenting the two different assessment approaches was twofold: first, to illustrate that different orientations can yield a brief assessment and second, to succinctly outline contrasting but potentially complementary approaches in hopes of perpetuating an eclecticism that is characteristic of many brief therapy approaches. Although it may be best to rely on one assessment strategy as one's primary approach, aspects of different approaches can often be successfully combined. To a large degree Budman and Gurman's (1988) and the behavioral approaches described are complementary. For example, once a therapist identifies a focus such as "interpersonal conflicts" from Budman and Gurman's list, behavioral strategies can be used to concretely specify the dimensions of the problem. Similarly, a brief-oriented behaviorist might borrow the concept of developmental dysynchrony to better conceptualize why certain problem issues are especially salient to a given person at a certain life stage. Budman and Gurman's and behavioral strategies are useful for brief assessment and are quite compatible with one another. Together, they make a particularly good combination for an abbreviated assessment. In no way do they represent the only or even the best approaches for a particular therapist, however. The thesis of this book is that most therapists can adapt their preferred assessment and treatment styles to a brief format if properly motivated. This chapter analyzed the assessment process, offered some models of brief assessment for those who might wish to borrow from these models, and illustrated some general principles of assessment abbreviation. The process of identifying a treatment focus is a critical part of assessment, and is presented in the next chapter. It will provide further assistance in assessment abbreviation.

Chapter Six

Establishing a Brief Therapy Focus

ORIENTATION TO A NARROW FOCUS

Rationale

The treatment focus identifies what a therapist and client will work on in treatment. Almost all brief therapy authors and advocates cite a *narrow* focus as the most important component of brief therapy, primarily because there is only enough time to deal with a single and narrow issue or two in a brief time frame. There are other important reasons why a narrow focus is an essential part of effective brief treatment, however. One of the critical contributions of the narrow focus is treatment efficiency: with all client and therapist attention directed at one target, very high levels of concentrated effort can be used. Each digression into alternative foci or treatment themes not only consumes the time required for discussion of the new theme, but it interrupts the momentum directed at the preceding theme. Additional time is then required to review the old theme and "gear up" the direction of resources toward it when it is returned to. Assessment is also far more efficient if only a single issue is assessed in depth.

Expectation of treatment benefit, a predictor of positive treatment outcome (Garfield, 1986), may also be enhanced by use of a narrow focus. Both client and therapist are aware that single, narrow issues have a greater chance of successful treatment than multiple or broad issues, mainly because client and therapist have an easier time maintaining a high level of motivation and expectation of success. The successful progression toward ameliorating an issue also provides reinforcement for continued work on that issue.

Lastly, single, narrow themes are more compatible with most clients' treatment goals and conceptualization of the treatment process—most clients desire and expect treatment to focus on circumscribed and modest goals directed at current life problems (cf., Chapter Two). In sum, maintenance of a narrow focus permits therapy to be brief, contributes to treatment and assessment efficiency and expectation of benefit, and is compatible with client goals.

It is important that therapists accept that successful resolution of a narrow focus is a legitimate function of psychotherapy even though broader or more ambitious treatment foci might be pursued under ideal circumstances (i.e., when the client has the desire and resources to pursue them). It is helpful for the brief therapist to remember that resolution of a circumscribed problem can be of very significant benefit to the client and may represent the only treatment option for the majority of clients. With this orientation, focus establishment is seen as the key ingredient of a beneficial treatment that can be enthusiastically pursued.

Therapist acceptance of limiting the focus may be facilitated by keeping in mind that one's basic therapy theory and treatment style can (and should) be retained during brief therapy. This means that narrow focus selection can be a natural variation of what therapists normally do in standard therapy. Treatment abbreviation is not especially difficult to accomplish: the ability of most readers to effectively adapt their therapy to the brief format will be apparent as the technique chapters progress. It is important for readers to be aware of their capacity to provide a unique form of help within the constraints of the briefer format. Most therapists can adapt to brief treatment without special training; the purpose of this book is to make the adaptation faster and better.

FOCUSING IN STANDARD THERAPY

Identification of a treatment focus occurs in all treatment. In standard therapy, the focusing can be done in many ways. Several relatively discrete problems may be identified, then treated either sequentially or simultaneously. Or a more basic problem (conceptualized as character issues, styles of life, general response patterns, errors in logic, or any number of constructs derived from the different therapy schools) may be identified as the cause of several symptoms and treated as the focus. Importance is not placed on a single narrow problem focus because of an implicit assumption that *all* or many problems will be treated eventually. In standard therapy, focusing is often done implicitly and issues are dealt with as they need attention. While the therapist may attempt to deal with one identified issue at a time, there is less emphasis on staying with the same issue from session to session. Indeed, sessions may often begin with an invitation to create a new focus, that is, by asking the client "what would you like to discuss today?" (e.g., Martin, 1983). Because specific problems are construed as part of an overall "problem package" that is the general treatment target, there is a freedom to deal with each problem that emerges, and even as it emerges.

FOCUSING IN BRIEF THERAPY

The General Strategy

The treatment focus is far narrower in brief therapy than in standard therapy. There is no assumption that all specific problems or basic character-type problems will be addressed. Typically, a single relatively circumscribed problem or two will be identified as the treatment target. These are problems almost always highly salient to the client and their resolution is sufficient for the client and brief therapist to regard treatment as complete.

The orientation of the *client* to a narrow brief therapy focus versus the broader or multiple foci selected in standard therapy presents an interesting contrast. Often the client presents a particular life problem that the therapist attributes to a more general client pattern. For example, a client who is upset over conflict with her mother may be aggressive and demanding of both her mother and other people. In standard therapy, the therapist typically tries to address both the general behavior (in this case, being aggressive and demanding of others) and the specific instance of its expression with the mother. In brief therapy, the therapist is more likely to limit treatment to the single conflict with the mother (while perhaps hoping for generalization to other situations). As noted in Chapter Two, clients are usually more interested in dealing with the narrower conceptualization of the problem, regarding it as highly salient and its resolution a sufficient treatment goal. Clients often have little interest in the broader problem and typically terminate before it can be successfully treated. This makes brief therapy a much more natural process for the client and consequently entails less therapist effort to orient (or cajole) clients to the treatment focus and goals. In this respect, brief therapy is easier to pursue than standard therapy (though not at all effort*less*, since the therapist must maintain a high degree of focus and activity).

A narrow focus can be fairly easy to maintain throughout treatment. Staying on focus is aided by the facts that the limited focus is compatible with clients' own conceptualizations of problems and it provides a simple, straightforward structure to the therapy session. Establishment and maintenance of a focus are not intrinsically difficult to do. However, there is a common obstacle when staying with a narrow focus: clinicians' reluctance to accept that certain client problems will not be addressed in treatment. This makes traditionally trained therapists uncomfortable; they often feel they are being negligent if they do not attempt to fix all client problems. The effective brief therapist copes with this concern by realizing that the typical client attends enough sessions to deal with only one or two issues and that the greatest progress is usually attained in the earliest sessions, i.e., the therapist must remain mindful of the core of the pragmatic, ethical, and humanitarian rationales for brief therapy described in Chapters One and Two (a review of this material is encouraged for readers who have skipped the early chapters of this book). The explicit negotiation of treatment focus with the client, described later in this chapter, can also reduce therapist concerns about neglecting important client problems. Perhaps the ultimate way to cope with this is to ignore any external constraints on treatment duration and use *client preferences* as a means of identifying treatment focus and duration. In the great majority of cases, the client's chosen treatment focus and duration will be within the time frame of a brief therapy, i.e., the notion of cheating the client will be rendered moot if client preferences are heeded.

Characteristics of an Appropriate Focus

A focus should be defined in clear, specific terms that are understandable and meaningful to the client. Use of assessment procedures (such as those discussed in Chapter Five) that yield client information that is concrete, present-centered, and problem-focused is the first step in focus identification. Use of vague, idiosyncratic, or metaphorical constructs impede this process and should be avoided when discussing a focus with clients. If you find such constructs useful in your theorizing you need to either ensure your theoretical language is easily grasped and accepted by the client or translate it to language that is. There is not enough time to indoctrinate brief therapy clients with complex jargon-filled conceptualizations—they need to make sense immediately to clients in brief therapy.

The focus will often be the client's presenting problem or an issue highly related to it. It will almost always be an issue that is instantly recognized by the client as a salient problem.

Focus Priorities

Clients occasionally describe a single, narrowly focused issue as their presenting problem at the beginning of treatment: for example, enuresis in an otherwise fairly well-adjusted child. Such problems are an appropriate brief therapy focus. Much more often clients present numerous symptoms, complaints, and problems. Selection of a focus becomes more difficult as problems increase in number, complexity, and pervasiveness. A general strategy is to simplify focusing by using the following "narrowness" hierarchy for identifying a focus: (1) a single, circumscribed problem; (2) life crisis; (3) behavioral or emotional dysfunction; and (4) personality-relevant problems. Each of these is elaborated below. Brief therapy becomes more difficult as the hierarchy is descended, so it is useful to conceptualize a problem at it simplest (numerically lowest) level.

- A *single, circumscribed problem* can occur in otherwise well-functioning individuals. Unlike a life crisis, there is no general upset and disorganization when such problems are present. Interpersonal conflict with a single individual, childhood noncompliance with certain parental commands, and job stress are examples. Once it is established that other areas of functioning are adequate, single and relatively simple problems are appropriate brief therapy foci. When these are presented, therapists often hunt for additional problems or broader ("deeper") problem determinants in order to make the course of treatment adequately substantial from the *therapist's* perspective. Therapists often feel that their work is insignificant or "not really therapy" if they only deal with simple problems. Clients do not have this perspective–they are especially pleased if simple presenting problems can be successfully treated in a short time, and quite prepared to terminate treatment at that point.

- A *life crisis* is a very upsetting situation that has proven refractory to the client's customary and even novel coping responses. Although a single event or situation may create a crisis, its effects are typically broad and very disruptive of many aspects of functioning. The conceptualization and treatment of problems as crises is greatly facilitated by familiarity with the crisis intervention model (cf., Caplan, 1964; Slaikeu, 1984). Clients with DSM V Codes, Adjustment Disorders, and some cases of depression are common examples of problems that are sometimes precipitated by crises, so that the crisis is an appropriate focus. Even when experienced by an individual with more pervasive problems (e.g., behavioral/emotional symptoms or personality disorders) a life crisis can sometimes be an appropriate treatment focus.

- *Behavioral or emotional dysfunction* refers to problematic behaviors and emotions that exist independent of crises, including: predisposition to emotional overresponding such as anxiety, anger, and some cases of depression; behavioral habits such as overeating; and combinations of emotional and behavioral symptoms, such as some cases of psychosexual dysfunctions. In brief therapy, such problems may need to be further narrowed by identifying the situation in which the symptoms are most problematic. For example, an individual with performance anxiety in social, sexual, and test-taking situations would be asked which of these was most important. Sometimes this narrowing is not necessary since the client often identifies this more narrowly defined expression of the problem as the presenting problem. Often the severity of behavioral/emotional symptoms is worsened by a life situation. Such cases can sometimes be conceptualized and treated as a life crisis. For example, if the previously described anxious client entered treatment because of high anxiety in a new work setting, this could be conceptualized as a life crisis.

This group of problems is obviously broad. The diverse problems within this group have differing and often complex determinants. Their placement in a group does not suggest a common etiology or treatment course, rather, they are placed together for the sole purpose of simplifying the focus selection process.

- *Personality* per se is not a suitable brief therapy focus, although the various problems associated with it can be. To derive an appropriate focus for someone with pervasive personality problems, further narrowing must be done. Personality disordered clients often decide to enter treatment when a life situation worsens an aspect of their pervasively dysfunctional behavior. This could be conceptualized as a crisis and selected as a treatment focus. This skill of narrowing a focus while cognizant of other problems *that will not be addressed* in treatment is often needed in brief therapy even when personality problems are not present.

NARROWING THE FOCUS WHEN MULTIPLE PROBLEMS ARE PRESENT

Which Focus Is Best?

When multiple or pervasive problems are present, it can be very anxiety-provoking for the therapist if s/he assumes there is only one "right" focus to select. This concern can be reduced by the realization that identification of a treatment focus is a rather arbitrary process that is only moderately influenced by the information supplied by the client; other important influences include the therapist's own personality, preferred theory, perceived skills, and general analytical skills. As a consequence, a number of different issues can be appropriately selected as a focus for a given case. Outcome research in general and brief therapy outcome research in particular (Bloom, 1992; Koss & Butcher, 1986) suggests that *there is no single necessary problem conceptualization or focus needed for successful treatment of a given client.* In reality, there are as many brief therapies as there are theories of psychopathology, and each is potentially effective with a given case: different foci selected for treatment by different therapists can result in successful treatment for a given case.

Theoretical Orientation and Focus

As with standard therapy, brief therapists begin with their basic theory and intuition in selecting the general treatment focus. The therapist's theory is less influential in brief therapy focus selection, however; the client's problem conceptualization and the nature of the presenting problem is usually more influential in determining brief than standard therapy focus. In standard therapy, the presumed cause of the presenting problem (and, supposedly, other problems) is often selected as the focus. Depending on orientation, these foci may be conceptualized as irrational beliefs, weak egos, maladaptive conditioning, incongruence between the self and experience, and other theory-derived constructs. This strategy for focus selection is feasible in standard therapy because, theoretically, if one treats such foci thoroughly enough, then a range of problems will eventually diminish. If one does not pursue the diminishment of a wide range of problems, however, the mandate to pursue the theory-identified focus is lessened, especially if there is a high cost (in treatment time) for this pursuit. When the focus narrows, therapists often relinquish equating focus with theory-derived treatment mandates. While theory still influences the *understanding* of a problem in brief therapy, it has less influence on focus and treatment technique selection. This may be one reason that brief therapists often seem more eclectic than standard therapists. This eclecticism is reflected in brief therapy texts, which are typically an amalgam of theory and technique (cf., Preface). My own observation of case presentations also supports the more pragmatic, eclectic approach to treatment taken by brief therapists: in general, when a case is presented to a group of clinicians with diverse orientations, there is often disagreement about treatment conceptualization, focus, and technique; however, in *brief therapy* case presentations, clinicians often reach a quick consensus, especially regarding treatment focus.

Psychotherapists receive considerable training in the identification of treatment targets, or foci. That training usually emphasizes a comprehensive assessment of client adjustment and identification of all problems. There is an implicit assumption that a good therapist will then attempt to deal with all or most of the client problems. Traditionally, good therapy has been synonymous with this accurate identification and successful treatment of all important problems (cf., Bloom, 1992). Narrowing the focus for brief therapy can be difficult for many therapists because it turns this traditional approach inside out: good brief therapy often entails deciding which *one* or two problems among many will be treated and what is the *minimal* improvement acceptable to the client. Procedurally this is not a difficult skill to master. The difficulty is in overcoming training that equates treatment comprehensiveness and perfectionism with treatment goodness. It is helpful to remember that the issue is not whether therapists will deprive clients of needed treatment but whether we will provide *the most help possible within the time allotted*.

A Key Question

Research on client expectations and dropout (reviewed in Chapter Two) clearly shows that a narrow focus is very compatible with clients' orientations to treatment. Empathizing with that client view of treatment can be an important step toward achieving an appropriately narrow focus. Focus identification can often be reduced to the following question: "What needs to be accomplished in order for the client to no longer feel a need for treatment?" That question accomplishment often suggests the treatment focus and goals.

Choosing Among Multiple Problems

When a client has multiple problems (or a general characteristic that yields many problems) focus selection is facilitated if relatively discrete problems are identified and roughly ranked regarding

- severity,
- client priority for treatment,
- need for immediate attention,
- potential for improvement, and
- treatment cost (in time, inconvenience, and money).

After considering these issues, a single problem or focus often emerges as the likely treatment target. As often, two or three foci emerge. Negotiation and discussion with the client should then be used to identify the priority focus. This discussion should include frank, explicit statements by the therapist regarding the considerations cited above regarding severity, potential for improvement, and cost. I urge therapists to consider and share with clients the research (depicted in Chapter Two) that shows that most treatment impact occurs early–that like many other educational processes, there appears to be a steep learning curve in psychotherapy. This further contributes to the selection of a narrow focus since clients will often select the surer success odds associated with a narrow focus. (Note that the process described here selects the focus or treatment issue. Selection of goals desired within the focal issue entails a separate negotiation process, described in Chapter Seven.)

A process similar to that just described (excluding reference to the steep improvement curve) often takes place in standard therapy. One difference is that, with brief therapy, the narrowing process is much more extreme. For example, consider a client who has multiple problems, including emotional lability in many interpersonal and evaluative/performance situations. A focus on general emotional lability is usually too broad. A focus on the single relationship or two most important and disrupted by client emotionality would be sufficiently narrow and appropriate for brief therapy. This illustrates the narrowing process in brief therapy.

PRACTICE EXERCISE

One of the greatest difficulties for all clinicians is to accept that some client problems will not be addressed in treatment. The experience of this phenomenon is quite different in brief and standard treatment. Standard therapists are typically faced with this prospect *after* an assessment, treatment plan, and therapy have been devised based on an assumption (or hope) that treatment would persist long enough to address most or "basic" client problems; often it does not last that long, but is terminated early and prematurely by dropping out. In brief therapy, acceptance of this treatment limitation occurs at the inception of treatment, when assessment and treatment planning are *designed* to be compatible with duration limitations imposed by reimbursement policies, client preferences, or other factors. In many ways it is easier to design a comprehensive treatment plan than to make, up front, the difficult decision regarding what to treat and what not to treat from among several valid treatment issues. In the latter case, the therapist takes partial responsibility for negotiation of a narrow focus and modest goals rather than default that selection to the client when s/he drops out or fails to comply with therapist recommendations.

In standard therapy, the main planning task is to identify the comprehensive range of treatment issues and associated techniques. In brief therapy, the task is to select from among all the potential issues the single issue or two that will most help the client. The exercises that follow will orient therapists to the latter task.

Step 1. Select a case with which you are familiar that warrants standard therapy, i.e., 20 or more sessions directed at pervasive or multiple problems. Consider what your treatment plan would be (or was, if you are recalling your own case) under conditions of unlimited sessions.

Step 2. Pretend this client can attend only ten sessions due to circumstances outside of his or the agency's control, e.g., the client is moving to a rural area without mental health resources in ten weeks. Consider what benefit you could provide with a more limited focus in only ten sessions. When considering benefit, remember that many of the common elements of both standard psychotherapy (Garfield, 1980; Prochaska, 1984) and brief therapy (see Chapter Four and Eight) are independent of theory-driven techniques and can occur within the first few sessions. For example, providing the explanation or conceptualization of a problem, predicting its typical course, exploring its meaning for the client, identifying client strengths, "depathologizing" or "normalizing" certain symptoms, and providing acceptance, warmth, and support can all be accomplished to some degree in the first session or two! Remember that therapist understanding, confidence, and encouragement, considered by clients as the most helpful aspects of psychotherapy (Sloane et al., 1975), can also be communicated within a couple of sessions.

Step 3. Now consider the focus you would select for that client if you could only treat for a total of five sessions. Consider the benefit you could provide in five sessions, remembering the common elements achievable in a few sessions. Think of the task this way: if you did everything right and used every possible resource at your and the client's disposal, could you be helpful in five sessions?

Step 4. Imagine reviewing treatment options from Steps 1, 2, and 3 (including potential benefits, costs, and number of sessions) with your client dispassionately and without prejudice. Remember to discuss the steep "learning curve" associated with psychotherapy, i.e., that research indicates a high probability of modest benefit within a few visits but a lower probability of the same rate of benefit with extra sessions. If you asked the client to select a duration preference (from treatment in Steps 1, 2, and 3), what do you think it would be?

The foregoing characterizes what typically goes on during brief therapy. The therapist thoroughly considers a cost-benefit analysis *for the client* for a range of treatment durations. To further understand the process, apply Steps 1 through 3 to other cases. Then consider what benefit could be achieved and what focus would be likely for three sessions, then two, then one for each case. (See Chapter Seven for the portrayal of goal options for treatment courses of differing durations for the same case.)

In brief therapy, the lowest number of sessions and narrowest focus are not always chosen or recommended, but the therapist *dares to consider them*, i.e., to assume the possibility of some benefit in a very brief time and communicate the cost-benefit ratio (and foci) of differing treatment durations to the client. Durations that are less than optimal are fully considered and seriously discussed because *they are likely to occur for most cases.* Remember that about one-third of clients terminate after only a few sessions regardless of third-party payers' policies or treatment cost, and that willingness to provide help in this time frame may offer such clients their only hope of help.

The selection of a focus is only one step in the treatment abbreviation process. Negotiation of limited treatment goals, discussed in the next chapter, further abbreviates treatment.

The general focusing guidelines and strategies presented so far are summarized below. They are best understood in the context of their use in the case example that follows the outline.

FOCUS SUMMARY

A. Orientation/Attitude

    1. Resolution of a narrow focus can

        a. Be a significant contribution to a client's mental health

        b. Fit well with a client's treatment preferences

        c. Save the client money and time

        d. Provide help in a short time

        e. Possibly be all a client can afford

    2. Basic theory and therapy style is relied on in selecting a narrow focus

B. Strategies/Techniques

    1. Eschew attempts to solve all problems or change personality

    2. General characteristics of an appropriate narrow focus are

        a. Definable in clear, specific terms

        b. Often the presenting problem or highly related to it

        c. Readily perceived by the client as a desirable focus

    3. The Focus Hierarchy

    Consider each of these as a focus:

        a. Simple, circumscribed problem

        b. Life crisis

c. Behavioral or emotional symptoms

d. Personality

4. Focusing when problems are pervasive or multiple

    a. Use your theory and intuition to conceptualize the case

    b. Pay attention to client priorities

    c. Ask "What needs to be accomplished in order for the client to no long feel a need for treatment?"

    d. For each of several potential foci, consider:
        i. Severity
        ii. Need for immediate assistance
        iii. Potential for improvement
        iv. Cost (in money, time, inconvenience)
        v. Client priority

5. If the above process fails to narrow potential foci to a single best choice, share *likely (not hoped for)* duration and outcomes for different foci with the client. Be very honest, citing outcome research findings when known.

6. Dare to consider and discuss what might be achievable in very brief treatment.

INTEGRATION OF ASSESSMENT, CASE CONCEPTUALIZATION, AND FOCUSING WITH A CASE EXAMPLE

Earlier it was noted that assessment, case conceptualization, and focusing are highly interrelated processes. Familiarity with the brief therapy procedures used in all three is prerequisite for doing any one of them well. Now that all three have been described, their application to a case example is possible. The major activities illustrated with this exercise are establishment and narrowing of the focus. It will be clear, however, that assessment and conceptualization skills described in Chapter Five are prerequisites to establishment of a focus.

There are two purposes to the case example. The first is to illustrate how a case of brief therapy is likely to proceed if the strategies recommended in this book are followed. The second is to provide a practice exercise for the reader. To do this, the reader is prompted at strategic points to consider how s/he might proceed with the case. The steps involved in assessment, conceptualization, and focus establishment are described in their normal sequence of occurrence in the first session so that readers can consider how they might proceed at each step.

The case example was created for this book—it does not depict a real client. It does accurately depict the nature of cases and their brief treatments, however. This particular case is of only moderate severity and, because it lends itself to a relatively simple brief treatment, is a straightforward training case. Readers who prefer a more challenging or an additional case are referred to Case #2 in Appendix A.

Case One

This client called the clinic asking for treatment of depression and "being miserable." That information, basic demographic information, and the fact that the client's insurance covered ten sessions was all that was known before the first (90-minute) session depicted below.

Initial Description

Bob is a 36-year-old man who summarized his reason for seeking treatment as a "mid-life crisis" and stated that his life was "out of control." Further questions (derived from the assessment techniques recommended in Chapter Five) revealed the following concerns:

- A weight gain of 20 lbs. in the past four months. Bob had been proud of his former athletic condition.
- Dissatisfaction with work stemming from conflict with his supervisor, who restricts the quality of his work by emphasizing quantity (he does ad and print layouts for a local newspaper);

these conflicts have resulted in frequent arguments with the supervisor and threats to quit work.
- Inability to begin his Master's thesis. Coursework was completed one year ago and the thesis topic was approved six months ago. Lack of an M.A. in his field (art) restricts his job mobility.
- Recently Bob's romantic partner accepted a job offer in another state after discussing it with Bob. They decided he would accompany her when she moved in four months (she receives her MBA in four months). Bob is anxious about the move, and is especially concerned that he will be dependent on his partner financially for a time after the move. Bob is now questioning his commitment to her because of his anxiety about moving.

These concerns have resulted in high anxiety and depression, with symptoms of sleep difficulties, overeating, and irritability with others, especially Bob's boss and partner. Bob has been living with his partner (and has been monogamous) for over a year. His current relationship is the longest relationship he has had in the past five years, though he has had others of shorter duration. He had been married from age 23 to 31; that marriage ended in an uncontested divorce.

Further Assessment

The above symptom summary (obtained in the first 30 minutes of Session One) would probably be provided by Bob to almost all brief therapists. The particular areas of inquiry addressed by different brief therapists would vary somewhat at this point. Readers should consider the questions they would pose to Bob at this point. One possible set of subsequent inquiries is presented next.

Why Now?

Bob's visit was precipitated by the fact that his partner recently accepted a job offer in a distant city, intensifying unresolved conflicts in Bob's relationship, career, and education. In addition, his lack of progress on his thesis over the past six months has raised concerns that he might never complete it. Bob feels that the impending move has placed a deadline on his thesis completion and increased his anxiety about it.

Other Questions

The following standard questions, likely to be asked by most therapists, were addressed next:

> Is there suicide risk?
> Has Bob been in treatment before?
> What was his adjustment previous to this episode?

The therapist was forming hypotheses about diagnosis at this point, and so asked questions relevant to the following:

> Does Bob suffer from major depression?
> Has Bob had chronic depressive symptoms indicative of Dysthymic Disorder?
> Is there alcohol or drug abuse?

The therapist's personal implicit view of emotional problems prompted the following issues to also be addressed:

> Is Bob highly autonomically arousable?
> Is Bob "neurotic"?
> Does Bob have "commitment phobia"?

Each therapist reading about the case probably has additional questions about Bob. Responses to the above questions revealed the following: Bob was not a suicide risk and had no history or current problem with drug/alcohol abuse. He had been in treatment once before, while a college undergraduate at age 21. He had about eight sessions at his college counseling center, precipitated by distress over choosing a major and a relationship breakup. Since that time, adjustment had been acceptable though Bob has a general tendency to be indecisive, procrastinate, and overreact emotionally. He had been quite happy and well-adjusted with his single lifestyle. Bob did not quite meet the criteria for Major Depressive Episode; a rather severe and complicated Adjustment Disorder was a more accurate diagnosis. Due to Bob's tendency to overreact emotionally, procrastinate, and exhibit some mild histrionic behavior, some might consider him mildly "neurotic" as well. Some might have classified him with a Borderline Personality Disorder.

Suitability for Brief Therapy

Although Bob was feeling great subjective distress and had a complicated set of problems, his case was suitable for brief therapy. Factors that made the case especially suitable, and even a potential candidate for *very* brief therapy, included his lack of suicide risk, previous acceptable adjustment, and lack of drug/alcohol abuse.

Case Conceptualization and Problem Focus

Before contemplating brief therapy, the reader should consider a traditional (long-term) focus for this case. The numerous possible foci include Bob's:

a. "neurotic" personality
b. general interpersonal assertiveness, and/or problem-solving skills
c. apparent "fear of success" and immaturity
d. general avoidance of relationship commitment
e. irrational beliefs

There may be additional foci considered by the reader.

All issues are too broad for brief therapy although some *aspect* of each could be a brief therapy focus. Bob clearly has many problems that are potential brief therapy foci. Some logical method for focus selection must be used to choose from among the many possibilities. Each therapist's own theory of problem behavior and general analytical skills will provide a starting point for focus selection. For some therapists, especially those with an inclination toward conceptualizing problems as discrete (though perhaps interrelated) entities, a narrow focus may be "intuitively" identified at this point. For most therapists, however, some further effort must be devoted to focus selection. Most readers will have some hunches regarding what they might select as a focus at this point, but will need further client questions answered before proceeding. The following describes some methods for focus identification. They are not presented as universal rules for focusing, but simply as a helpful guide for some and a counterpoint for the formulations of others. Mainly, this is an attempt to articulate what typically occurs implicitly in brief therapy so the reader can see the process and appreciate the similarities and differences with standard therapy.

Use of the decision hierarchy presented earlier may be helpful for problem conceptualization and focus selection. This entails conceptualizing Bob's plight as one of the following: (1) a single circumscribed problem; (2) a life situation that created a crisis; (3) behavioral or emotional symptoms not due primarily to situational determinants; or (4) "personality." In applying this to Bob, his is clearly not a simple circumscribed problem (#1), nor are his problems behavioral or emotional symptoms without major situational influence (#3), although there are certainly emotional and behavioral aspects to his problems. There *are* several life situations (#2) that together contribute to his plight. These include the supervisor conflicts, thesis difficulties, indecision about commitment precipitated by his partner's new job, and generally being out of step with his expected life stage regarding career and relationship, i.e., a "developmental dysynchrony" (cf., Budman & Gurman, 1988). These are all sufficiently circumscribed to serve as brief therapy foci. (There are also personality characteristics present (#4) that warrant treatment, but, as usual, these are not sufficiently circumscribed to serve as a brief therapy focus.) Unfortunately, there are too many potential foci in this list to all be dealt with in a brief therapy–a common situation. One or two themes or problems need to be identified from this list of problem situation.

As noted earlier, consideration of a number of factors, listed below, can sometimes help narrow the focus to a single issue:

- problem severity
- client priority for treatment
- immediacy or urgency for attention to a problem
- potential for improvement, and
- treatment time and effort required

Client Contribution to Focus Identification

At this stage, information on all these factors except client focus priority is available for all the identified problem life situations. No particular problem stands out as the obvious treatment choice, however. Our information fails to clearly identify or even eliminate a focus. This makes client priority, which is always important, particularly important. As in standard therapy, it is useful to provide the client with tentative problem conceptualization before asking about treatment priorities. This allows the therapist to assess if his or her view of the problem makes sense to the client and provides a common frame of reference for discussing treatment issues. Toward this end, the therapist proposed that the "mid-life crisis" seemed at least partly due to confluence of the four life situations (supervisor conflicts, thesis, commitment, developmental dysynchrony). After a brief discussion and Bob's agreement, the therapist noted that these problems were not discrete, unrelated events, but that each contributed to the others. The sum of their effects was that Bob felt like his life was out of control. The therapist then provided the conceptualization depicted in Figures 6.1 and 6.2 as rationales for considering the thesis and commitment issues as possible foci, showing that many symptoms derived from these two issues and their interactions.

Figure 6.1 shows that thesis resolution has the potential to eliminate or improve many of Bob's concerns, i.e., it may be what needs to be accomplished so Bob no longer feels a need for treatment. In addition to reducing symptoms as depicted in Figure 6.1, thesis completion would help Bob regain some measure of control over at least one aspect of his life.

Similarly, the commitment issue also contributed to many symptoms and its resolution had the potential to reduce many problems, as depicted in Figure 6.2.

The therapist acknowledged that other issues might be priorities for Bob, however, and urged Bob to consider other issues. After some discussion, Bob concluded that the thesis and commitment issues were highest priorities. Since both foci would entail considerable effort, only one could be addressed in brief therapy, at least initially. Toward the end of Session One, the therapist asked Bob to

Figure 6.1. Problem Conceptualization A

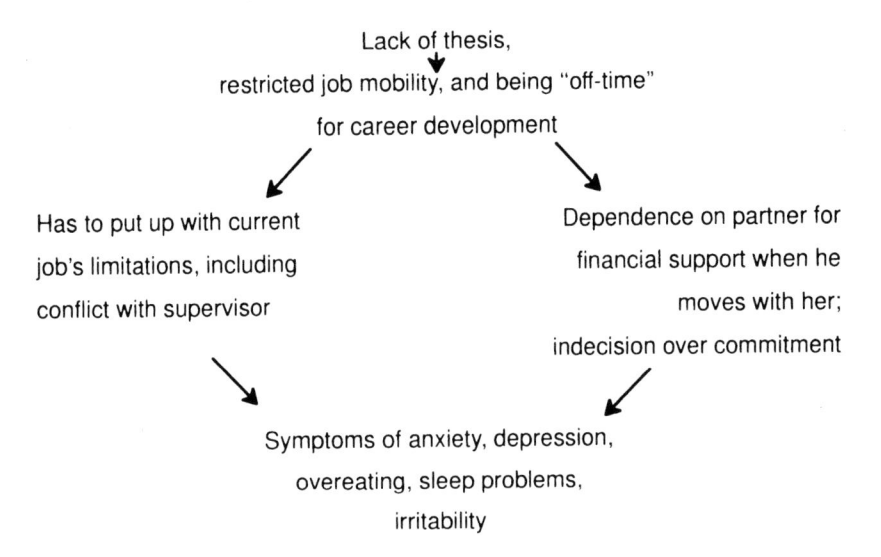

Lack of thesis, restricted job mobility, and being "off-time" for career development

↙ ↘

Has to put up with current job's limitations, including conflict with supervisor

Dependence on partner for financial support when he moves with her; indecision over commitment

↘ ↙

Symptoms of anxiety, depression, overeating, sleep problems, irritability

Figure 6.2. Problem Conceptualization B

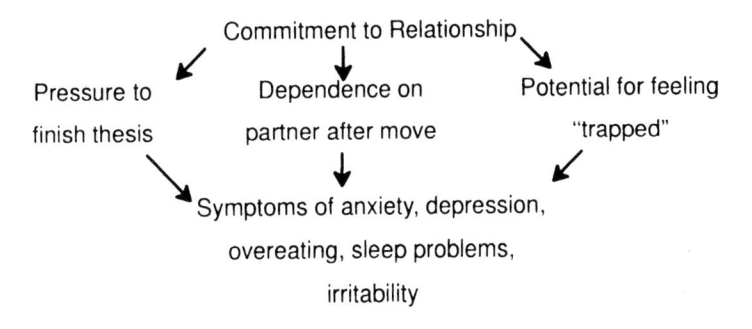

Commitment to Relationship

↙ ↓ ↘

Pressure to finish thesis

Dependence on partner after move

Potential for feeling "trapped"

↘ ↓ ↙

Symptoms of anxiety, depression, overeating, sleep problems, irritability

---

take the next week to consider which of the two issues he thought most important and preferred to deal with first. Bob was reassured that the focus not chosen (as well as others that might emerge) could be addressed later if Bob desired to spend the extra time and money.

At the beginning of the second session, Bob reported that he preferred focusing on the thesis; he noted the greater immediacy of this issue and the fact that it could simplify the commitment issue, since its resolution might eliminate Bob's financial dependency on his lover. It also had a higher probability of a straightforward resolution than the commitment issue. This, then, became the primary treatment focus.

Analysis of Session One

General Accomplishments

Several things were accomplished at this first session: assessment; development and sharing of a problem conceptualization; and narrowing the focus to two possibilities. In addition, rapport was established—empathic understanding, acceptance, reflection of emotion, and other basic counseling techniques were exhibited by the therapist. While all this was important, another task remained for the first session that was *as important* as any of those just cited: the therapist was obligated to try to provide some form of crisis relief. The last 20 minutes of the first session were reserved for this. By that point the therapist had some confidence in his conceptualization of the case (which was essentially what is depicted in Figures 6.1 and 6.2) and was in a position to explore several short-term interventions for alleviating Bob's high stress and insomnia. Because this aspect of the first session is better categorized as "treatment" rather than assessment/conceptualization/focusing, these interventions will be described in Chapter Eight, which deals with adapting standard treatment techniques to the brief format.

Three points merit discussion regarding the chosen focus.

- *Focus Flexibility.* First, although the selected focus will probably be the target of most treatment efforts, the therapy is not a slave to the focus. If a more important focus emerges or crises develop, new topics will be dealt with. And as time allows and conditions warrant, other issues associated with the focus may also be treated.
- *The "Best" Focus.* Second, while the focus selected was derived by a logical process, it is not the only or perhaps even the best possible treatment issue. Other foci may have been selected by other therapists and may have provided the client

with as much or perhaps greater benefit. Even given this therapist's approach, it is clear that the commitment issue also warranted being a focus. Case assessment by a therapist with a different approach may have yielded a quite different set of initial foci considerations and a very different chosen focus. *What was probably most important about this process with Bob was that the focus selection process made sense to both Bob and the therapist: an issue considered important to both was selected, and the therapist had some confidence in his ability to treat the focus chosen.*

- *Narrow vs. Trivial Foci.* Third, it would be easy for a traditional therapist to dismiss the chosen focus, dealing with the thesis, as a trivial issue. The therapist did not view this as trivial at all, however. As Figure 6.1 shows, lack of a thesis is related to many of the client's current concerns, including his career, relationship, self-esteem, and stage of life dysynchrony. The therapist recognized that any and all of these, as well as more basic personality factors, could be appropriate treatment foci. Indeed, he realized that the thesis may have been important only because of the client's vulnerabilities in these other areas. Nevertheless, the thesis problem adversely affected all these areas and was therefore important.

If Bob were interested in longer treatment these other issues could be addressed, but the therapist had many reasons to believe that addressing a single narrow focus would be a better bet for helping Bob: (a) the thesis was an apparent crisis precipitant, so on humanitarian grounds it made sense to alleviate the immediate stress by trying to alleviate one of its obvious causes; (b) insurance covered only ten sessions; (c) Bob wanted no more than ten sessions; (d) there was an urgency to finishing the thesis—if it were not completed in four months it would interfere with the move with his partner; (e) his previous (free) treatment had lasted only eight sessions suggesting a client tolerance of only brief treatment; and (f) base attendance rates show that the odds are that *any* client will probably terminate by the tenth visit. In addition, the therapist was quite confident that he could help the client cope with the thesis and was less optimistic about successfully resolving such general functioning as personality "neurosis," or even relationship commitment. Longer treatment was not precluded: if the thesis problem became resolved, the client could consider addressing other issues in light of some treatment success. Finally, it should be recognized that addressing the thesis issue would not be a simple matter of outlining the steps to completing a thesis. Bob was an intelligent, successful student who knew how to do that. Therapy would entail finding out what blocked the thesis project and addressing those obstacles. The therapist realized that a wide range of psychological variables might need to be addressed along the way, including: the possible function of the thesis as an escape from the relationship and adult career responsibilities; coping with the anxiety provoked by doing the project and risking failure; Bob's difficulty asserting the need to devote time for the project to his lover and boss; expectations Bob had for himself and others; and his general problem-solving skills. Different therapists might focus on different obstacles or deal with these same obstacles in various ways. Although a variety of other issues might be improved as a by-product of dealing with the thesis, they would be of ancillary benefit to the main treatment issue, coping with the thesis. While mindful of these possible benefits, the brief therapist keeps the focus on the main issue, realizing the high probability of benefit in that area if kept in focus.

Once a focus is identified, treatment goals—the level of progress within the focal area that must be achieved for treatment to be considered successful—need to be addressed. The negotiation of treatment goals is an important step and is considered in the next chapter.

Chapter Seven

Negotiating Treatment Goals

Treatment goals are the specific outcomes desired for the focal issue; their negotiation is typically the next logical therapy task after a focus is established. Addressing treatment goals presents an opportunity for the therapist to get a sense of the client's outcome aspirations and for the therapist and client to generate a mutually defined criterion for termination.

Goal identification is pursued with the same spirit as focus selection: there is a collaboration and identification with the client's perspective on goals, often for modest goals rather than perfect functioning within the focal area. Pursuit of modest goals produces many of the same benefits as adherence to a narrow focus, because both have the effect of restricting and clarifying the scope of treatment. Modest though significant goals are beneficial in brief therapy because: modest goals are more quickly achieved than ambitious ones; they are also often recognized as imminently achievable by both client and therapist, thereby promoting optimism and high levels of effort; perhaps most important, the goals are often chosen as the result of an explicit negotiation between client and therapist, ensuring that the scope of treatment will be compatible with *client preferences*. This contributes to brief therapy being "consumer-oriented" and may accelerate the development of a positive client-therapist relationship. As will be shown in the strategy and techniques section of this chapter, the client typically has even more influence on the identification of goals than the identification of a focus: client preference is the primary determinant of brief therapy goals.

Important sharing of information occurs during the goal negotiation process. Therapists provide valuable information regarding therapy's potential benefits, its limitations, and the time and cost required to achieve various goals. Clients are asked to share their treatment aspirations, the investment they are prepared to make in treatment, and the value they place on various treatment outcomes. These types of revelations carry some risk but have the potential to contribute to a strong alliance and a feeling of trust between client and therapist.

GOAL SELECTION IN STANDARD THERAPY

Therapists often have difficulty distinguishing focus and goals because, in standard therapy, there is much overlap between them and little functional need to make their distinction. Theory-driven approaches to standard treatment often translate a focus into theory-related phenomena (such as illogical beliefs or early childhood experiences) which, if addressed by the treatment dictates of the theory, will achieve an implicit goal of normal adjustment. More generally, there is often the assumption that normal functioning–a "cure"–is the treatment goal (see Chapter Two for detailed documentation of therapists' typically ambitious goals and pursuit of "cures"). In other words, treatment goals are often implicit in standard therapy. When goals are implied, it reduces the client's opportunity to participate in their selection. A client's standard for acceptable functioning in an area may be very different from the therapist's: clients typically seek improvement in problems rather than their "cure," personality change, or general improvement in functioning.

In Chapter Six, it was shown that a general focus, too, is often implicit in standard therapy–that is, that all problems will be addressed at some point in therapy. The attitude that "we'll eventually take care of everything" in therapy makes a distinction between focus and goal unnecessary. Even when specific foci are identified, they are often so broad (e.g., "self-esteem," "emotionality," "interpersonal behavior," "anxiety") that specifying particular goals is difficult. Behavior therapy, with its highly specific foci and goals, is somewhat of an exception. But here too foci and goals are broadened by selecting multiple foci and goals or general skills as goals.

Whether the treatment goal is implicit or explicit, in standard therapy it is usually assumed that the ultimate impact of treatment will be witnessed by the therapist—treatment is prolonged until satisfactory adjustment is observed by the therapist. Even when therapists acknowledge that a limited level of improvement is all that can be realistically expected for a client, they expect to monitor the achievement of that improvement.

GOAL NEGOTIATION IN BRIEF THERAPY

In contrast to standard therapy, brief therapy treatment goals are usually clearly distinguished from the focus, are explicit, and are negotiated with (or even solicited from) the client.

Perhaps the most important thing about the use of explicit goals in brief therapy is that *the goal negotiation process presents the best opportunity to frankly discuss treatment duration with the client.* Selection of a focus sometimes entails discussion of duration, but consideration of duration is secondary to clinical needs when selecting a focus. The client's pain and therapist's conceptualization expertise are major determinants of focus selection. Duration is more easily isolated as an issue when discussing goals. Because different goals often require different numbers of sessions, goal negotiation gives the therapist a perfect opportunity to link goals and treatment duration. Indeed, if certain goal negotiation strategies are employed (as outlined below) it almost forces the therapist to estimate treatment duration for various goals. For a therapist who is not used to discussing duration or is uncomfortable doing so, practicing the goal negotiation strategies described in this chapter provides an opportunity to become comfortable discussing duration with clients. Rather than limiting treatment by some arbitrary session cutoff, briefer treatment can be a logical treatment chosen by most clients when certain focus and goal selection strategies are used.

In brief therapy a distinction is often made between the goal to be achieved by the end of treatment and the long-term impact of treatment. It is accepted that treatment may start a process or identify a plan of action that is to be carried out *after termination*. If the therapist and client are confident that the process or plan will continue (admittedly a big "if"), the therapist does not always have to be a witness to their effects. This takes a little of the glory out of therapy since the therapist is not present to get credit as improvement continues, but this approach can greatly abbreviate treatment, saving considerable time and money for the client.

GOAL CHARACTERISTICS

Earlier it was noted that it is easy to confuse goals with foci, or even with treatment techniques. This section identifies the components of goals in order to clearly describe their nature and distinguish them from related clinical phenomena.

In brief therapy there is quite a specific meaning to the interrelated terms "focus," "goal," and "treatment." A focus is the issue or theme that will be addressed in treatment–the client's "problem." The goal is the desired change within the focal issue. Treatments are the means used to deal with the focus and achieve goals.

One of the clearest descriptions of how to identify treatment goals has been provided by Egan (1982). His guidelines for establishing goals are very helpful for our purposes. He recommends that six criteria be used in goal establishment. They have been adapted for our purposes:

1. Goals should be *achievements rather than programs* or treatment techniques. Systematic desensitization, communication of empathy, and correction of illogical beliefs are examples of treatment programs or techniques rather than clinical achievements. They are the *means* toward the ends of treatment goals. Use of the behavioral assessment strategies described in Chapter Five are helpful here: a goal can often be best depicted as an overt change in behavior within the focal issue as it occurs outside of the session.
2. Goals should be *clear, specific,* and *verifiable*. They are best stated in terms clear enough that the client, therapist, or any independent observer could identify their presence. The client and therapist should have no trouble knowing when they have been achieved. Overt behaviors are clear and verifiable, and thus are usually the preferred types of goals. Even if cognitive or intrapsychic goals are desired, their behavioral manifestations can usually be identified and used as goals.

3. Goals need to be *realistic*. In brief therapy, this often means modest though substantial.
4. Goals should be *adequate* to meet a client's satisfaction. It is easy to achieve realistic goals that are trivial; the difficulty is in achieving goals that are realistic but substantial.
5. A reasonable *time frame* should be *specified* for the accomplishment of goals. This is critical in brief therapy and is fully discussed later in this chapter.
6. Goals should be based on *client*, rather than therapist, *choices*. This is a theme that is presented throughout this chapter.

GOAL IDENTIFICATION AND NEGOTIATION STRATEGIES

Identification of a narrow focus is the first step in securing an appropriate brief therapy goal. As in standard therapy, identification of a focus identifies an implicit goal of improvement in the focal area. If the focus is limited, the goals will be too. Usually the nature and extent of improvement should be further specified, however.

The general strategy is to try to identify the level of functioning within the chosen focus that is adequate for the client. The client's perspective on this is paramount. Questions such as "What would you like to accomplish [within the focal area]?" or "What would be acceptable [in the focal area]?" can help keep goal-seeking oriented to the client. The brief therapist must often overcome traditional training in order to be adequately client-oriented. In standard treatment, the therapist has much more influence on determination of client goals. When goals are implicit, it encourages the therapist to keep scheduling sessions until his or her standard for acceptable adjustment is met.

In traditional treatment, theoretical orientation often dictates that techniques become goals. Theoretical dogma often insists that certain techniques are necessary and sufficient for improved adjustment; when this happens, the application of technique becomes the goal since it is believed that their use inevitably creates good adjustment. In brief therapy, the attainment of theory-dictated goals such as to "think more rationally" or "make the unconscious conscious" are not acceptable goals. The brief therapist is not an agent of a school of therapy who automatically pursues the ideal state of adjustment dictated by theory. Instead, the brief therapist may adhere to a theory's tenets regarding causes of behavior and behavior change, but s/he uses these and probably other techniques in order to achieve the client's goals. The brief therapist is mindful that techniques are a means to achieving goals rather than goals themselves.

ESTIMATION OF TREATMENT DURATIONS FOR DIFFERENT GOAL LEVELS

Perhaps the single best technique for putting oneself into a brief therapy mode is to consider two or more goals that vary in ambition level for the same focus. If a therapist dispassionately describes the goals and their estimated treatment duration, s/he puts the client in some measure of control of goal selection. For therapists not previously trained in brief therapy, a technique such as this is often necessary in order to change the ingrained habit of selecting goals for the client.

Going through the process of considering various goals and their estimated treatment durations is often an excellent way to approach treatment as a brief therapist. It makes one aware that a variety of goals are possible and reasonable for a given focus, thus preventing "locking into" an assumed best goal level. It makes one conscious of the relationship between treatment benefit and duration (cost). By openly discussing the goal options with the client, it reveals that clients often prefer goals that are different from those assumed necessary by therapists and empowers clients to choose such goals. These benefits to goal negotiation make it important to pursue this issue in depth. It should be recognized, however, that this goal negotiation process is easier when goals and foci have overt behavioral referents. So this process will be more straightforward with, for example, child conduct problems and the case study's thesis struggle than cases of grieving and existential foci. When therapists tend to conceptualize cases primarily in existential or psychodynamic terms, it is more difficult to identify clear-cut goals and their estimated durations, but that does not preclude use of this goal negotiation exercise: for any therapist, consideration of goal negotiation heightens one's awareness of the importance of goal flexibility, the cost/benefit ratio of their treatments, and the importance of client goal preferences. Practice of the goal negotiation technique is a good way to become more comfortable with an attitude about therapy which is useful for all brief therapy cases, whether or not gradations of specific goals for a particular focus are clearly identified.

As in focus selection, the process of goal negotiation is done best if the therapist can objectively acknowledge that higher cost and longer time is required to achieve more ambitious goals and that disproportionately greater effort is usually required to achieve smaller increments in improvement as goals become more ambitious. In other words, the therapist should be mindful of the relationship of treatment duration to outcome presented in Chapter Two and, when appropriate, present this information to the client. The ideal circumstance is for the therapist to truly align with a client's preference for modest goals, to sympathize with the client's desire to "get a good deal" (a lot of help for the time invested–a higher benefit/cost ratio), and to accept that a goal is worthwhile if it is acceptable to the client even if it is less than the therapist would prefer. The underlying rationale, as always in brief therapy, is that a large percentage of clients inevitably terminate early and a large percentage of them will get as much help from brief therapy as they would from longer treatment. They are best served by modest goals, compatible with a brief duration.

Goal Negotiation Technique

The technique of goal negotiation is simple and straightforward once one accepts the premise that it is reasonable to consider varying levels of goals, including modest ones, and their estimated durations. Initial orientation to the client's aspirations can usually be best accomplished by asking questions (after the focus is identified, of course) such as "What would you like to accomplish [in the focal area]?" or "What would be acceptable for you [in the focal area]?" or "How would you know things are o.k. [in the focal area]?" More generally, the therapist needs to know *what needs to be accomplished in the focal area so that the client will no longer feel a need for treatment.*

Questions such as the foregoing usually provide some general idea of what the client wants to accomplish. It is tempting for a traditionally trained therapist to stop the goal-setting process at this stage (after a general goal is identified) since therapists are normally trained to stop the goal identification process at or even before this point. The real test for a brief therapist is to go to the next stage–to force a revelation of specific *alternative* goal levels and accept the "risk" that the client will accept the more modest one! This is much more a psychological than a procedural barrier for the therapist. Procedurally, one simply says something like "I think I have some sense of what you want to accomplish, but let me see if I can get a little clearer idea. Let me describe two treatment options, then tell me which one is closer to what you would like. How would it be if you [describe first goal scenario]? Many clients find that this sort of goal takes about x to y sessions. Or would you rather [describe the more modest alternative goal]? This would probably take about y to z sessions." The same procedure can be extended to describe three or more goal levels when appropriate.

There are three critical corollaries to the above process. First, it is important to describe two significantly different but usually contiguous goal levels that basically define the upper and lower functioning levels of the broad long-term treatment goal. Second, it needs to be clear that the estimated session range needed to achieve the various goals are rough estimates (*never* implied guarantees). When treatment is unlimited in time, there is usually no need to estimate treatment duration; as a result, traditional therapists are not well practiced in the estimation of treatment duration for attaining various goals. Therapists in training are often cautioned to not be so bold as to make such predictions lest they fail, imply a guarantee, or create a "resistance target" for the client. For these reasons, therapists often find the prospect of treatment duration estimation problematic. This turns out to be a needless concern the great majority of the time; brief therapists can become quite good at this with modest amounts of practice. There is a simple explanation for this, traceable to the fact that about 80 percent of all clients terminate by the fifteenth session whether or not treatment is designed to be brief. Once one becomes sensitive to this, you spend most of your time estimating treatments for the few very constrained treatment ranges that exist within one to 15 sessions i.e., one to five, six to ten, 11 to 15, or some similar ranges. As one accumulates experience in brief treatment for particular disorders, it becomes quite easy to identify different goals for contiguous treatment ranges. For example, it becomes pretty easy to estimate the improvement possible for a particular noncompliant hyperactive child in six to eight vs. eight to 12 sessions. Everything that one knows about a particular client is combined with one's experience and with knowledge about treatment of a particular type of problem in order to make such estimates. If a particular client is difficult to size up in this regard, one does not make a duration estimate.

The best way to predict durations for particular goals is to rely on one's own accumulated case histories in brief treatment. The problem, of course, is finding some way of making the estimates *before* one has accumulated a lengthy brief therapy record or when treating problems one has not previously encountered. There are two resources for these situations. The first is to consult with a supervisor, consultant, or colleague who has experience in the brief treatment of such cases. The second is to be familiar with the research literature on the impact of various treatments for particular disorders—almost all of the outcome studies published in refereed journals are of a brief duration, whether or not identified as brief therapy! As the mental health professions move toward the use of empirically demonstrated treatments (Chambless, 1993), this latter recommendation represents one more practical reason for becoming familiar with the outcome literature. Excellent textbook resources are now available that summarize this outcome information for treatments of various adult disorders (see T.R. Giles' [1993] *Handbook of Effective Psychotherapy*) and childhood disorders (see Morris and Kratochwill [1991] *The Practice of Child Therapy*). The ideal brief therapist is extremely knowledgeable about psychotherapy and psychopathology in general, so this familiarity with outcome research should be part of the brief therapist's continuing education anyway. When familiar with the outcome literatures for various disorders, it is possible to tell a client something like this: "substantial research has been done on problems like yours and the average client usually improves significantly in about [x to y] sessions. My best guess is that [Goal One] probably could be accomplished in about [x-2] to [x+2] sessions and [Goal Two] probably could be accomplished in about [y-2] to [y+2] sessions." Obviously, the form of expression in this book sounds somewhat stilted out of context; in practice this is incorporated into each clinician's personal style and goes very smoothly. It should be noted that, when done correctly, the estimating of treatment duration for goals enhances the therapist's credibility (it informs the client that you really know something about the client's problem), and reduces client anxiety (it informs the client that s/he is not alone in suffering such problems and that established treatment strategies are available).

It was noted earlier that there are three aspects to the process of treatment goal and duration estimation. The first two have now been covered (the identification of significantly different goal levels and the skill of estimating durations). The third is an awareness of the *probabilities* of achieving varying levels of goals. Generally, it is unethical to identify specific probabilities for goal attainment (e.g., to claim that 85 percent of clients achieve . . .) unless substantial replicated research warrants such claims. It is usually safest and most accurate to use broad estimates, referring, for example, to what "the majority of clients" achieve. When it comes to identifying two different goal levels it is often true that the probabilities for their achievement varies. When the goals are fairly similar, little needs to be said about differential probabilities because the research literature is not very specific about the odds of achieving similar levels of outcomes. But when one goal is far more ambitious than another and outside of what has been empirically demonstrated to be a likely outcome, the therapist must be very cautious about predicting such ambitious success levels–such predictions may be unethical (Ethical Principles of Psychologists and Code of Conduct, Standard 3.03; APA, 1992). The outcome literature (see review in Chapter Two) generally shows a higher probability of achieving modest rather than ambitious goals, so this differential probability should usually be acknowledged (unless there is empirical evidence to the contrary) when substantially different goal levels are discussed. Obviously we are speaking here of cases where both goals are adequate to meet a client's needs. The acknowledgment of the higher probability of reaching modest goals is yet one more way that there is compatibility among the brief therapist's knowledge of the treatment literature, professional ethics, and alliance with client preferences.

The discussion thus far has only considered probabilities for various outcomes in a general way, based on research and personal observation of cases aggregated for problem and diagnostic groups. Obviously the therapist must also consider all other information predictive of outcome when making such estimations, including the client's resources, motivation, problem severity, and the presence of multiple problems.

Goal Attainment and Termination

Goals can provide termination criteria; when met, termination should be considered. The identification of clear goals thus simplifies the termination process. Quite often, due to the nature of the client's problems or the theoretical/conceptualization style of the therapist, clear goals are not set during early stages of treatment. When no observable goal referents are identified, the client's internal state must be used as the termination criterion. Rather than continue treatment until a (usually unattainable) "cure" or perfect functioning occurs, the brief therapist periodically assesses the acceptability of the client's status. A simple way to do this is to ask the client to "Consider how things are going for you now. If they were like this when you first entered treatment, would you have sought treatment?" Or, more cautiously, "If things were like this when you first entered treatment, what would you have wanted to address in treatment?" Asking such questions as improvement occurs is advisable even when clear goals have been set because client goals can change during treatment. Questions like the above often allow the client to express feelings of satisfaction with current adjustment and can open up a discussion of termination. In such cases clients are likely to reveal that they have been (privately) wondering about the need for continued treatment and contemplating termination. By bringing up the topic, the therapist gives the client permission to discuss it openly. Often clients are reluctant to bring up termination when the therapist continues to dwell on problems because the implication is that such problems should be treated. The therapist's psychological dominance of the therapy scenario can inhibit the client from expressing the opinion that therapy has met his or her need. Such a situation can set up treatment dropout.

Goal Negotiation Summary

1. Distinguish goals from focus and treatment techniques.
2. Remember the characteristics of goals; they are
    a) achievements, not programs
    b) clear, specific, and verifiable
    c) realistic
    d) adequate
    e) include a specified time frame
    f) based on client preferences
3. The general orientation: what should be accomplished so that the client no longer feels a need for treatment?
4. Describe two different goal levels and their estimated treatment duration; if adequate information is available, identify the probabilities of achieving different goals.
5. Be prepared to accept a client's preference for more modest goals.
6. Consider goal negotiation early in treatment; if not feasible early, reconsider goal negotiation in middle or later stages of treatment as a termination criterion.
7. As significant improvement occurs and you get a sense that the client is approaching an acceptable level of adjustment (using his or her standards), consider assessing the acceptability of current adjustment by asking "If your current adjustment (in the focal area) were in effect at the time you decided to enter treatment, would you have sought treatment?" When the answer is an unequivocal "no," consider discussing if goals have been met and termination is appropriate.
8. Be prepared for the client to prefer termination once the treatment plan is set in motion but before ultimate goals are accomplished.

CASE EXAMPLE: NEGOTIATING GOALS AND TREATMENT DURATION

The case of Bob, who initially described himself as having a mid-life crisis, was introduced in Chapter Six. After several specific problems and issues were identified, the therapist and client agreed to focus treatment on Bob's inability to complete his Master's thesis because this caused him great subjective distress and contributed to job, relationship, and "adult developmental" problems.

After selection of a focus, goals are often identified within the focal area. This section will address how goals and treatment duration could be negotiated with Bob. Recall that a brief crisis intervention successfully reduced Bob's acute distress in the first session. This exercise begins in Session Two, after the thesis focus has been identified and Bob has described improved sleep and lowered stress. (Most of Sessions One and Two were devoted to assessment/ conceptualization, focusing, goal selection, and treatment planning. The *interventions* that were directly applied to Bob's sleep and somatic symptoms during Sessions One and Two, a sort of crisis intervention, are described along with the rest of treatment implementation in Chapter Eight.)

A word of warning before proceeding: Bob's case was selected for presentation because of the relatively simple and clear foci and goals that can be identified. Other cases present far different sorts of foci and goals. Readers who prefer a more complex case are referred to the summarized treatment of "Mary" in Appendix A.

Implicit vs. Explicit Goal-Setting

There was considerable discussion of the rationale for selecting the thesis difficulties as a focus during Session One, at which time a conceptualization of the thesis relation to other problems was presented to the client. At the beginning of Session Two, Bob verified that this was the issue he wanted to address in treatment and provided a convincing justification (consistent with Figure 6.1) for wanting to work on this issue. Goals are selected based on the assumption that their attainment will result in improved adjustment as reflected in a wide range of subjective and objective indicators. Obviously, these indicators need continual monitoring throughout treatment. For Bob, these indicators include his particular job, relationship, and mid-life existential issues as well as the emotional symptoms of stress, sleep disturbance, and weight gain. The theorized relationship between the thesis and adjustment indicators was shown in Figure 6.1. If the presumed relationship between goal attainment in the focal issue and improvement in these indicators of adjustment did not materialize, treatment would have had to be reconceptualized. The reader is reminded that the focus and goals referred to in this case presentation represent the wider range of adjustment indicators just described.

It was clear from the context of discussions about the thesis that Bob wanted to complete the thesis and graduate—this was an implicit ultimate treatment goal. In standard therapy clinicians might not see a need to do further goal specification—they would expect to keep the client in treatment until all relevant problems were resolved and the thesis completed. It would be very tempting to assume that identification of a focus with such an obvious implicit goal renders further goal discussion unnecessary. Such an assumption would detract from the efficiency and effectiveness of brief therapy, however, for brief therapy goal negotiation provides an opportunity to (a) distinguish between the ultimate impact of treatment and the goal to be accomplished within the duration of treatment, and (b) openly discuss treatment duration options.

The strategies outlined in the Goal Negotiation Summary were used to address Bob's treatment goals. Goal negotiation ensued with the assumption that Bob wanted to complete the thesis, though not necessarily before the termination of treatment. As is typical of brief therapy, the therapist was mindful of the distinction between progress observed during the course of treatment and the ultimate (post-treatment) impact of therapy. (As in the case example's exercise for identifying a focus, it might be most useful to consider how you would treat Bob if he were your case. Assume that you and he have selected the thesis as a major brief treatment focus and you are about to begin the second session after Session One was conducted as described in the previous chapter.)

Goal Alternatives

Although the therapist was most comfortable with selecting completion of the thesis—passing an oral defense and acceptance of a final thesis draft by his committee—as the treatment goal, he realized that Bob might feel confident of his ability to complete the thesis at some earlier point and might prefer to terminate treatment then. The therapist's task at this stage was to generate a range of approximations to thesis completion and present reasonable ones to Bob as goal alternatives. The following were generated by the therapist:

1. Successful oral defense of the thesis.
2. Submission of the written thesis and the scheduling of an oral defense.
3. Submission of an initial thesis draft to the committee.
4. Creation of a thesis outline and completion of 50 percent of the thesis content.
5. Identify the components of the thesis; identify and successfully cope with obstacles to working on the thesis; and completion of 25 percent of the thesis as an indicator that Bob is "well on his way" to completing the thesis.
6. Identify the components of the thesis; identify the obstacles to working on the thesis; creation of a plan of action for coping with the obstacles; work on the thesis for two weeks while successfully coping with previous obstacles.
7. Same as # 6 except that the goal is met with creation of the coping plan.

Notice that the description of these goals adheres to the (Egan, 1982) guidelines for goals. They are all: achievements rather than therapy techniques or programs; specific and verifiable; and realistic. The issues of their adequacy for the client and the time frames required for their attainment could only be addressed after more information was obtained about the nature of Bob's thesis, and Bob's experiences with it. This required a second round of assessment, one that addressed the treatment focus. These assessment stages are characteristic of brief therapy: an initial assessment is done in order to identify a focus, followed by a detailed assessment of the focal issue.

Assessment of the Focal Issue

Goal negotiation and, more broadly, treatment planning, requires that the therapist have a thorough understanding of the focal issue. For Bob's case, this meant learning about the nature of the thesis and why Bob has been unable to work on it successfully—an assessment and conceptualization of the focal issue. The relatively narrow and specific nature of Bob's particular focus—the thesis—was especially amenable to a focal assessment, for the nature of the thesis could be assessed independent of Bob's experience and characteristics. The therapist asked questions likely to be asked by many therapists:

- What is the nature of Bob's academic discipline?
- Are there specialty areas in his discipline and, if so, what is his specialty area?
- What is the usual form and content of a thesis in Bob's field?
- Are there separate parts to the thesis?
- About how long does it take to complete each part under normal conditions?
- Has Bob created a thesis proposal?
  - How difficult was that to do?
  - How well was it received by his thesis chairperson?
- How does Bob get along with his thesis chairperson?

These and similar questions produced the following information: Bob's thesis proposal had been very well received by his thesis chair, with whom Bob got along very well. Bob's specialty area was lithography. A thesis in this area had to be in a very structured format: it was composed of six distinct parts, each related to a step in the lithography process (e.g., creation of an original sketch, etching the sketch on a metal plate, etc.). Each part took about the same amount of effort; Bob estimated that about 15 to 20 hours would be needed to do each part. The therapist, incidentally, had virtually no prior knowledge of lithography or academic art programs.

Bob's Experience with the Focal Issue

Once the nature of the thesis was understood, Bob's experiences and problems with it needed to be assessed. The therapist asked:

- Does Bob like the thesis topic?
- Is he competent in this area?
- What kinds of experiences has he had with similar tasks?
- What seems to be the problem doing the thesis?
- What happens when (and if) he attempts to work on the thesis?

These and related questions yielded the following:

Although Bob was quite competent in his thesis topic and was quite interested in it, he had a tendency to put off difficult academic tasks (procrastination) such as long term papers. He had several "Incomplete" grades in undergraduate courses that required term papers or similar projects. With the thesis and similar tasks he became easily distracted, redirecting his energy to task-irrelevant activity. He easily succumbed to available recreational activities when faced with tedious tasks. Much of this counter-productive behavior appeared mediated by anxiety. He generally became anxious when faced with such tasks and found that the anxiety increased the longer he delayed task completion. Engagement in recreation provided anxiety relief.

This particular task created great anxiety for Bob. It had all the general characteristics of tasks that usually elicited his anxiety: it was a long, difficult, and important job. Because he had delayed work on it for several months, the anxiety had worsened. And once there was a sort of deadline imposed by the move of his partner, the pressure and anxiety became very high. When Bob tried to work on it, he reported that his "mind went blank" except for anxiety-provoking and catastrophizing thoughts.

The information just described about Bob is the result of the particular questions asked; they provided a means of construing the thesis problem and a basis for treatment planning—conditions that allowed goal negotiation.

Goal Selection

The assessment information enabled the therapist to negotiate a goal from among those identified earlier. Given Bob's history of procrastinating, identification of a plan of action and completion of only a portion of the thesis (goal alternatives 4 to 7) seemed ill-advised. Discussion of option # 2 (completion of pre-orals draft and scheduling the orals) and #3 (submission of initial thesis draft) resulted in Bob choosing option #2: he felt that after completion of a polished draft and scheduling the orals, there would be "no turning back." In his department, the oral exam was usually an automatic approval of the project and only minor changes were typically required at that stage. The hard part was getting to the oral exam. The goal, then, was to get to that point.

Estimation of Treatment Duration

Recall that the thesis was composed of six parts, each of which required about 15 to 20 hours of work. After much discussion about Bob's work and recreation schedule, it appeared that he could devote about 15 to 20 hours per week to the thesis—enough time for one of the six thesis parts, if the obstacles to thesis work could be overcome. The therapist suspected that treatment would entail some further crisis intervention for his most upsetting somatic symptoms, problem-solving to set up a work routine, and coping with anxiety. A preliminary estimate of the treatment duration required to attain the selected goal was now possible because the therapist could do some treatment plan speculation. The therapist estimated that it would take about two sessions to get Bob to engage in sustained thesis work, and an additional two sessions to get him to be able to work productively for 15 to 20 hours per week. Once that was accomplished, weekly one-hour sessions might not be necessary. But one or more of the nonfocal problems (supervisor conflicts, partner/commitment issues, weight gain, emotional/somatic symptoms) might need further intervention during part of some sessions. So the therapist estimated that two to four sessions would be needed to get the thesis up to one part completed per week, followed by six sessions for monitoring the thesis and coping with Bob's anxiety and the other issues. Adding a session or two for thesis refinement and coping with orals anxiety led to an estimate of approximately eight to 11 sessions beyond Session One (i.e., a total treatment course of nine to 12 sessions).

Analysis of Session Two

General Accomplishments

Like the initial session, the second session of brief therapy tends to be "dense" and filled with several tasks. In Bob's case, the second session included the following: Bob's verification of his satisfaction with the focus chosen in Session One; further assessment and conceptualization of the focal issue; consideration of broad goal options; narrowing of goal options based on the focus assessment; estimation of the treatment duration for the selected goal; and discussion of goal options and selection of the treatment goal by Bob.

These are the treatment tasks typical of brief therapy's second session. In addition to these specific tasks of brief therapy, other more general therapy phenomena occurred: rapport was deepened by the therapist's continued empathy, acceptance, and demonstrations of interest through detailed questioning of Bob's behavior and feelings. In the first part of the session, the crisis intervention begun in Session One for Bob's somatic symptoms was continued also (this treatment aspect of Sessions One and Two is elaborated in the next chapter).

Let us consider the logical progression of brief therapy through the first two sessions as illustrated by Bob's treatment. The first session was primarily devoted to general descriptions of Bob's concerns, broad case conceptualization, identification of potential foci, and (tentative) focus selection. In the second session, there was further assessment of the focal issue and characteristics of Bob that were *directly relevant* to the focus, a conceptualization of the causes of the focal problem, identification of goal options and goal selection, and estimation of treatment duration. Over the first two sessions, assessment and conceptualization of problems were progressively narrowed, culminating in selection of a specific treatment goal and its duration estimation. In Chapter Four, the four key common factors in brief therapy were introduced; three of the four (assessment/conceptualization, focus establishment, goal negotiation) were accomplished by the end of Bob's second session. Aspects of the fourth, treatment implementation, were also introduced in the first two sessions. Clearly, the first, two sessions of brief therapy are very important.

The Timing of Goal Negotiation

Bob's problems were well-suited to an explicit negotiation of goals and their treatment durations early in treatment. As noted earlier in this chapter, that is not always the case. When clients are in severe crisis, especially, discussion of goals and/or treatment duration may communicate a threat of abandonment when the client's greatest need is to be reassured that the therapist is available *as much (and as long) as necessary to help overcome* the crisis. Clients with existential issues (e.g., grieving a death) are similar–discussions of goals and treatment durations might be insensitive early in treatment. Also, there are cases where there is little need to discuss goal options early because the client presents both a preferred goal (e.g., alleviation of depression) and a complicated set of determinants. In these and other cases where early (first or second session) goal/duration discussion is inadvisable, it is almost always true that a somewhat later (e.g., between the fourth and eighth sessions) discussion of goals/duration is advisable. By that time, crises have usually subsided, case complexities are better understood, and, more generally, the conditions that precluded earlier goal/duration discussions have diminished.

Appropriateness of Goals

Brief therapists consult extensively with clients about focus and goals before their selection and acknowledge that clients ultimately decide (by termination) when treatment is finished. But brief therapists also acknowledge their influence and responsibility in these areas. When goals are finally identified, the therapist obviously uses professional judgment to decide if a goal is conducive to good adjustment of the client. For Bob, the extensive case conceptualization in Session One (represented by the diagrams in Chapter Six) describes the therapist's "theory" of the link between the chosen focus (the thesis) and Bob's distress. Following this logic, it is obvious that completion of the thesis should alleviate much of Bob's distress, but this must be confirmed by the therapist's observations. The therapist also assumed professional responsibility for taking some short-cuts while considering goal alternatives: instead of discussing every one of the goal options on page 94, he eliminated some that he considered inadvisable and presented the two he deemed most appropriate for the client. If Bob had balked at these, the therapist would have been obligated to discuss other options while disclosing their benefits and risks.

Duration Estimation: Technique vs. Philosophy

The consumer benefits of explicit duration estimation and goal negotiation have been described throughout this chapter. It has also been noted that it is sometimes inappropriate to do this, especially very early in treatment. Even when the brief therapist declines to have an explicit discussion about goals and their treatment duration, however, it is important that s/he consider these issues from the beginning of treatment. This early therapist awareness of likely goals and their treatment durations is an important determinant of treatment brevity.

Goal Discussion as Treatment Planning

Much of Bob's second session was devoted to assessment of the focal issue—gaining an understanding of why Bob had trouble with his thesis and identification of Bob's potential coping resources. Discussion of goals forces the therapist to do preliminary treatment planning, since this is needed to consider what goals are achievable and how long their treatments would be. Goal discussion entails a contemplation of treatment but not necessarily its implementation. Bridging that gap by the adaptation of traditional treatment strategies to a brief format is the subject of the next chapter.

Chapter Eight

Treatment Implementation: Adapting Standard Psychotherapy Techniques to a Briefer Format

The emphasis in the last three chapters has been on ways to abbreviate treatment by narrowing its scope and broadening the collaboration between client and therapist when selecting treatment goals. This chapter addresses how to successfully apply treatment interventions within an abbreviated format.

This book attempts to be compatible with most approaches to treatment; it assumes that the great majority of approaches provide beneficial ways of understanding and treating problems, and that these can be adapted to a brief format. This ecumenicalism regarding treatment is a representation of a view of psychotherapy that claims that common treatment factors exist in most therapies and account for much of psychotherapy's impact. Terms such as "common factors" (Bergin & Garfield, 1994), "eclectic" (Garfield, 1980), "generic" (Orlinsky, Grawe, & Parks, 1994), "psychotherapy integration" (Norcross & Goldfried, 1992) and "transtheoretical" (Prochaska & DiClemente, 1984) have been used by various authors to express this view. This approach to understanding psychotherapy was partly inspired by findings that different treatments often produce similar outcomes for a given disorder (Lambert & Bergin, 1994). While there has been no clear empirical demonstration of precisely which of the conjectured commonalities account for psychotherapy's effects, Bergin and Garfield (1994) have identified three credible explanations for the similar outcomes phenomenon. The first is based on behavioral learning theories and contends that most treatments provide clients with the opportunity to unlearn dysfunctional responses and acquire beneficial ones. The second posits that the therapeutic relationship is psychotherapy's "active ingredient" when it is characterized by attributes such as warmth, empathy, and acceptance. The third focuses on the culturally defined role of the therapist as healer and persuader. It encompasses four subsystems: cathartic relief of affect; a rationale for explaining client problems; procedures for achieving improved ways of living; and faith in the healer.

Several specific (and often complex) systems for addressing the common factors in psychotherapy are addressed by authors such as those cited in the preceding paragraph. Consideration of how the common factor approach applies to brief therapy is important for the understanding of treatment technique in brief therapy. This book has emphasized common strategies for *abbreviating* treatment (e.g., by selection of a narrow treatment focus) thus far. It is also true that brief therapy advocates tend to recommend *interventions* that often have common elements, although the commonalities are often only revealed after treatment jargon is substituted by more generic language.

To illustrate this, let us consider two completely separate (and quite different) brief therapy approaches, Slaikeu's (1984) crisis therapy intended for use with a wide range of life crises, and Budman and Gurman's (1988) brief therapy of losses. It should be noted that, although both approaches identify themselves as eclectic, they derive from very different traditions. Slaikeu's is primarily associated with broad-based cognitive-behavioral approaches such as Arnold Lazarus's (1981) and Albert Ellis's (Ellis & Harper, 1975) work. Budman and Gurman's is more influenced by psychodynamic and existential approaches. Neither set of authors references the other in their books. Slaikeu (1984, pg. 138-139) emphasizes four tasks:

Task	Client Activity
Physical survival	Preserve life (prevent suicide, homicide) and maintain physical health.
Expression of feelings	Identify and express feelings related to crisis in a socially appropriate manner.

Cognitive mastery	(a) Develop reality-based understanding of the crisis event.
	(b) Understand relationship between crisis event and client beliefs, expectations, unfinished business, images, dreams, and goals for the future.
	(c) Adjust/change beliefs, self-image, and future plans in light of crisis event.
Behavioral/ Interpersonal Adjustments	Make changes in daily patterns of work, play, and relationships with people in light of crisis event(s).

Budman and Gurman (1988) identify five procedures in their treatment of losses:

1. Specifying and naming the relevant loss, exploring its meaning, and identifying for what other people besides the patient it is a loss.
2. Providing information about the frequent course of or response to this type of loss.
3. Encouraging a "regrieving" for the loss, both with the patient and with others who have suffered the loss in question.
4. Gaining some closure on the loss.
5. Addressing the loss in a social context. (pp. 82-83)

Both of these ostensibly unrelated approaches emphasize very similar content—the expression of feeling, exploration and understanding of the meaning of problem situations, and making interpersonal adjustments. It should not be too surprising that these brief therapies (as well as many others) overlap considerably with and can be understood in terms of the common factors ascribed to psychotherapy in general. Grencavage and Norcross (1990) have reviewed the literature concerned with common factors and have identified those factors most often cited. Compare their list, shown below, with Slaikeu's and Budman and Gurman's treatment outlines presented earlier:

1. The development of a *therapeutic alliance*.
2. The opportunity for *catharsis* or ventilation of problems.
3. The *acquisition and practice of new behaviors*.
4. Patient positive *expectations* and hope for improvement.
5. Beneficial *therapist qualities*, particularly the therapist's ability to cultivate hope and enhance the patient's positive expectancies.
6. Provision of a *rationale* that provides a plausible explanation for the patient's problems as well as procedures for resolving them. (pg. 49)

Almost all the treatment procedures described in Slaikeu's and Budman and Gurman's outlines are accounted for in Grencavage and Norcross's common factors. The degree of commonality illustrated by comparison of Slaikeu's and Budman and Gurman's therapies is representative of common therapy recommendations expressed by most brief therapy approaches. This analysis suggests that there are intervention commonalities among brief therapies that can be considered expressions of the factors common to *all* psychotherapies. My reading of the brief therapy literature finds certain factors that are both particularly common and especially helpful in *brief* treatment.

INTEGRATIVE MODEL FOR BRIEF THERAPY INTERVENTION

1. *Provision of immediate practical assistance and linkage to other resources (family, community, and professional) as warranted by clinical conditions.* This, of course, is one of the distinctive elements of crisis intervention. The practical help and linkage to other resources are also consistent with brief therapy's general goals of providing clients with as many resources as possible, especially if they are affordable, accessible, and part of a client's natural environment. This factor is consistent with the pragmatism of brief therapy–there is no disparagement of practical help as something reserved for assistants, technicians, or aides. The brief therapist is there to be helpful and acknowledges that practical help often can reduce problems more than purely psychological interventions.

Knowledge of local resources is critical to the provision of these interventions.

2. *Development of a therapeutic relationship.* This results largely from provision of the other procedures in this outline. Some research suggests that therapist expression of empathy, support, and caring, consistent with Rogerian (Rogers 1951, 1961) recommendations, contributes to the establishment of a therapeutic relationship and good outcome. In brief therapy, such therapist expressions usually occur in the process of doing other assessment or treatment procedures. Research suggests that high levels of therapist treatment activity are consistent with building a good therapeutic relationship (Sloane et al., 1975). Clinical tradition suggests that exploration of client feelings (see factor 4) is especially conducive to a therapeutic relationship.

3. *"Naming" the problem and describing its nature and probable course.* This and the two following factors are aspects of a larger issue, achieving a broad understanding, or cognitive mastery, of the problem situation. The "naming" referred to in this context is the therapist's provision of an *initial* orientation to the client problem that is derived from the therapist's special knowledge base. The naming may be accomplished with a diagnosis or some other rational means of categorizing a problem. The particular diagnostic/categorization system and affiliated theory is probably not especially important as long as it makes sense to the client, as suggested by Frank (1982). As treatment progresses, a detailed explanation of the cause of a client's plight usually emerges, along with a compatible set of techniques for alleviating the problem. This "naming" aspect of treatment refers to the simplest aspect of problem conceptualization, informing the client that his or her problem is a comprehensible phenomenon. It is the first step in changing the problem from being overwhelming, mysterious, and pervasive to being understandable, predictable, and controllable.

An additional benefit of this is that it enhances the therapist's credibility and therefore the client's expectation of benefit. Categorization can also delimit the scope of the problem, comforting the client with the information that the problem derives from certain specifiable antecedents and affects particular (not all) aspects of functioning. Consider, for example, the benefit that naming the problem and describing its nature can provide depressed clients who often see themselves as total failures, their world falling apart, and have no hope of improvement. Much benefit can occur by simply (empathically) informing such clients that: they have the clinical problem of depression, which is relatively common, well-researched, fairly well-understood, and treatable; our understanding of depression suggests that negative perceptions they describe of themselves, the world, and the future are predictable (normal) symptoms of depression rather than valid observations; and such perceptions, being symptoms, typically improve substantially over the initial weeks of treatment.

Describing the course of a problem condition is beneficial for all the same reasons I have just identified for "naming" a problem. In addition, the clinician is often able to provide the client with good news regarding the future of many conditions, since many emotional problems tend to improve on their own over time. The converse of this is also true: the therapist can "normalize" or "depathologize" symptoms that persist long after a problematic life situation by explaining that some symptoms normally persist for a period longer than many people anticipate.

4. *Exploration of feelings and the meaning of the situation for the client.* Clients inevitably have strong feelings and beliefs about their problems when they enter therapy. The expression of these thoughts and feelings allows the therapist to gain a fuller understanding of the client's view of and reaction to their plight. The articulation of these thoughts and feelings is often the first opportunity that the client has to systematically review them. This process, then, allows *both* client and therapist to gain some understanding of the emotional aspects of the problem situation. In the process, illogical beliefs may be voiced that can be later refuted by the client or therapist.

The emphasis in this factor is on the client's subjective, affectively influenced self-exploration. This is especially important when subjective, affect-laden material constitutes the essence of the client's problem, such as occurs with existential problems, grief reactions, and post-trauma stress. This sort of affect exploration is, of course, consistent with theories and therapies that emphasize the importance of regrieving when dealing with grief reactions (e.g., Klerman et al., 1984; Kübler-Ross, 1975; Worden, 1982) and, more generally, reviewing traumatic incidents (Blake et al., 1993).

5. *Putting the problem in perspective through attainment of intellectual understanding and rational appraisal.* This involves a logical, rather than subjective and emotional, appraisal of the problem. It is an extension of the theory-based view of the client's problem provided by the therapist when naming or diagnosing a problem. In this aspect of treatment, a more thorough explanation of the client's problems is provided, usually in a way that changes a client's beliefs. These changes may be accomplished in a variety of ways: for example, a direct disputation or replacement of problematic beliefs, such as occurs in cognitive therapies like Beck's (Beck et al., 1979) or Meichenbaum's (1985), or by showing the client that problematic behavior is motivated by previously unacknowledged (unconscious) conflicts.

The emphasis here is on the therapist's provision of a new way of viewing the problem and an associated way to change client views in a therapeutic manner. This goes beyond the simple problem naming described earlier–the focus is on changing specific ideas that are presumed to affect symptoms.

Much of what is therapeutic about rational appraisal, exploration of feelings and meaning, and naming the problem is that these procedures all provide the therapist with an opportunity to provide some sense of normalcy about the apparent abnormal experiences of clients. This can be especially important for clients fraught with anxiety or self-denigration about their conditions. Normalizing can be achieved by noting that their problem is *common* (not actually abnormal) or *understandable* given their circumstances.

6. *Problem solving.* Common factors 2 through 5 are primarily addressed within the therapy office, focusing as they do on cognitions, feelings, and the therapy relationship. Factors 6 and 7, like factor 1, address phenomena outside the office, typically preparing the client to take action. The understanding achieved in earlier steps often identifies problematic behaviors or relationships that contribute to the client's problem. In problem solving, the therapist functions as a consultant to assist in the creation of plans of action that are designed to improve a client's adjustment. The therapist's contribution may derive from his or her more objective view of the

client's plight, general analytic skills, theory-based prescriptions, or use of formal procedures designed to accomplish effective problem solving, such as the ones described by D'Zurilla and Goldfried (1971) and Nezu and Nezu (1989).

7. *Implementation of behavior change.* Problem solving typically entails analysis of problems and the identification of behavior changes to be enacted. Often such behavior change is difficult to do. Indeed, clients often present at the first session knowing that a presenting problem consists entirely of the failure to engage in a particular behavior. Treatment frequently entails the therapist's assistance in helping clients implement desired behavior changes. Attitude change accomplished by some of the other factors is sometimes adequate preparation for behavior change, but often other procedures are needed to induce behavior change. Psychotherapists use a wide range of other procedures for inducing change, including exhortation, paradoxical prescriptions, role-playing, and theory-based structured procedures such as systematic desensitization.

This "integrative model" section has been described in generic terms so that therapists with different approaches can recognize therapeutic elements that they provide; most therapists will probably acknowledge that much of what they try to accomplish is contained in this outline. The contents of the outline overlap considerably with the specific integration models cited earlier and incorporate much of the three general common factors explanations provided by Bergin and Garfield (1994).

The particular way that each component is expressed and the degree it is emphasized will vary among different brief therapists, of course. For example, item five–attainment of problem understanding–might primarily entail discussions of self-concept for some therapists and illogical beliefs for others. During a course of treatment, different therapists will emphasize different components; those with a psychodynamic or humanistic-existential approach would probably emphasize factor 4 (exploration of feeling and meaning) while cognitive-behaviorists would probably emphasize factor 6 (problem-solving) and factor 7 (behavior change). This model has a number of implications for brief treatment that will be described throughout this chapter. One of them is that the abbreviating activities of the first two sessions—assessment, case conceptualization, and selection of a focus and goals—contain important *therapeutic* elements.

ASSESSMENT/TREATMENT PLANNING VS. INTERVENTION: TREATMENT IN THE FIRST SESSION

This book has followed the tradition of separating what are normally considered pre-intervention therapy operations (e.g., assessment, case conceptualization, focus and goal selection) from actual treatment interventions. Inspection of the integrative model reveals that this can be a misleading distinction, for some of the common *therapeutic* elements of brief therapy (activities that reduce client upset) occur as part of assessment/conceptualization, focus selection, and goal negotiation. These latter three procedures typically entail naming the client's problem and describing its course (as part of shared problem conceptualization and focus selection), exploration of feelings and the meaning of the problem in an empathic relationship, and some degree of putting the problem in perspective. As illustrated by the case example in the last chapter, problem solving can be initiated during goal negotiation in the first or second session. When crisis intervention is part of treatment, behavior changes may be implemented as early as the first session.

It is important to be aware of these often subtle therapy acts in order to appreciate the contribution of activities during the first two sessions to the overall impact of brief therapy. It is obvious that these activities orient the client and therapist to the treatment by identifying what will be addressed in treatment (the focus) and the sorts of changes desired in the focal area (goals). But much more can and should be accomplished *therapeutically* during the first sessions of brief therapy: the abbreviating strategies discussed so far can be performed so that they themselves deliver therapeutic elements to the client, as summarized below. (The reader is referred to the Case Example sections of this book to see detailed illustrations of how this can be accomplished.)

Each of the abbreviating strategies described thus far presents opportunities for delivering particular therapy elements described in the integrative model. The assessment procedures described in earlier chapters provide an excellent opportunity to inquire about the feeling/meaning aspects of a problem (factor 4). Early brief therapy sessions are the natural time to commence such exploration for most clients.

Case conceptualization entails identifying problems, their causes, and effects (factor 3). This often provides a new perspective on problems (factor 5) and further exploration of their meaning for the client (factor 4).

The selection of a *focus* derives from the assessment and conceptualization, and therefore provides further opportunities to accomplish the therapeutic tasks of those phases (factors 3, 4, 5). The therapist has the chance to present the focal issue in a new light, providing opportunities for further understanding, exploration of feelings, and discussion of the nature of the problem and its likely course.

As was shown in the previous chapter, *goal-setting* often involves further assessment and conceptualization of the focal issue and therefore provides further opportunity to address components 3, 4, and 5. It also adds a new element: preliminary discussion of treatment goals and (covertly, if not overtly), therapist consideration of treatment plans to attain the goals. The latter involves preliminary problem solving by the therapist (factor 6) which can (and should) be shared with the client.

In summary, the brief assessment, conceptualization, focus selection, and goal negotiation procedures can be used to at least begin the provision of many therapeutic elements. Indeed, *all* of the therapeutic elements except the action-oriented ones (factors 1 and 7) *typically* should be addressed during the first session or two. Obviously the crisis-oriented element of factor 1 may also be addressed in the first session of some cases. The provision of these elements in early sessions is not inevitable, however, the therapist must purposefully exploit all (the numerous) opportunities for provision of therapy elements in order to deliver them in early sessions.

Therapist Self-Assessment

If it is true that common factors contribute to treatment impact, it seems that it would be desirable for a therapist to be competent in delivering all the various common factor treatment elements. This is one of the rationales for investigating psychotherapy integration (Arnkoff, Victor, & Glass, 1993). The finding that outcome is related to therapist skill × client problem interactions (Beutler, Machado, & Neufeldt, 1994) further underscores the desirability of therapist technique versatility. My own observations of therapists suggests that our personality and training influence us to emphasize some common factors more than others and, more important, to be variably skilled at doing these. Brief therapists need to be very competent so that they can deliver maximum help in a short time. That means that brief therapists must have all the treatment elements at their disposal, be aware of their importance, and be willing to use them. I encourage readers to seriously consider the degree to which they are able to use these different therapy tools and consider the possibility that improvement in the weaker areas might enhance their treatment. Therapists do not need to emphasize all these elements equally, however. Therapist style and skill will dictate more use of some treatment factors than others. The important question is not whether one is generally *inclined* to use a given treatment element, but if one *can* use it competently when it is called for. My own experience in trying to abbreviate treatment suggests that simple awareness of one's strengths and weaknesses and inclinations and disinclinations to use the various treatment elements in the Integrative Model can be an important first step in improving the breadth of one's treatment competencies. Self-improvement usually can be accomplished by technique-oriented reading (see relevant works in the Reference section), workshop attendance (see description of workshop impact in Chapter Ten), and special supervision (see Appendix B).

STRATEGIES FOR ADAPTING TRADITIONAL TECHNIQUES TO A BRIEF FORMAT

In the preceding sections it was shown that much therapy is provided in the first sessions while assessing, conceptualizing, and so on, and that this is enhanced by purposefully integrating common treatment elements with these abbreviating procedures. This was one way of adapting techniques already part of most therapists' repertoires to a brief format. In this section, three other ways to adapt techniques that you already possess to a brief format will be described. The first of these emphasizes the use of short-term treatment goals in every session. The second is a selected listing of psychotherapy techniques that seem especially well-suited to a brief treatment format. The third emphasizes general ways to introduce interventions in an abbreviated format.

Philosophy and Client Advocacy

This is a good point at which to revisit the philosophical/values issues described in Chapter Four. There it was noted that attitude about treatment is probably more important than technical skill in the effective conduct of brief therapy. The basic attitudinal orientation of the brief therapist is that of a client advocate–a professional who will take every step possible to help the client. The earlier section on "Therapist Self-Assessment" addressed the importance of therapist competence, flexibility, and breadth of skills in brief therapy. Client advocacy goes beyond such therapy technique issues, however: it requires the therapist's willingness to engage in activities outside of the realm of psychotherapy (but still within the mental health professional role) in order to help a client. The brief therapist should be aware of the community resources most likely to be needed by clients and ways to access them. Depending on the characteristics of one's clientele, this could include knowing: procedures/requirements for securing forms of public assistance such as Medicare, Medicaid, state welfare, Aid For Dependent Children, Legal Aid, vocational training, and child daycare; local policies/obligations for schools to provide psychological testing and services for children with special needs; criteria for admission or access to local mental health agencies, programs, and self-help groups; and self-help books that are useful for various client problems. The effective brief therapist is usually a good community psychologist and so typically has developed rapport with key community caregivers and has a list of their names and phone numbers.

SHORT-TERM GOALS

In the preceding chapter on goals, the emphasis was on what was to be accomplished by the end of treatment or some point after termination. Short-term goals refer to the subgoals that can be accomplished *during* a session or *between* sessions. In most brief therapy, these smaller goals often contribute to the long-term goals, but they also provide tangible benefit in the short run. They are often the actions and outcomes noted in each case note. In crisis intervention or one session therapy, the short-term goals are the primary treatment goals (though it may be hoped that other goals will be reached some time after termination).

Standard therapy typically orients clinicians to think of ambitious goals such as symptom removal, personality change, general improvement in functioning, and "cures." When short-term goals are discussed, they are typically conceived as building blocks of long-term goals; if they have immediate benefit, that is usually a chance by-product of the pursuit of ultimate goals (the exception being a crisis intervention, where immediate symptom relief is the goal). When short-term goals designed to alleviate problems or symptoms are identified, their achievement is often designed to take place over a period of weeks. Such a building-block style of short-term goals are often pursued in brief therapy also. In addition, however, short-term goals are identified that provide immediate help *at every visit*. Especially when the projected course of treatment is less than eight or so sessions (remember that this applies to a majority of clients in most settings), immediate assistance should be identified for each session.

There are a variety of ways that this short-term help can be provided. *First*, of course, is through the use of treatments that are fast-acting. Relaxation training, hypnosis, and some psychoactive medication are examples. *Second*, and less obvious, is through the use of communications that relieve distress directly. This includes "de-pathologizing" or "normalizing" client concerns, "naming the problem," direct advice, and simple support and reassurance. It has already been shown that assessment/conceptualization, focusing, and goal setting provide many opportunities for such interventions in early brief therapy sessions. *Third*, linkage to helpful community resources can also bring immediate relief.

A *fourth* means of providing rapid help is somewhat unique to brief therapy. It involves the relief associated with the accomplishment of major steps toward a proximal goal. Once an achievable and substantial goal has been identified in brief therapy, interventions that are steps toward that goal can bring immediate client relief if (a) a clear relationship between each step and the ultimate goal has been identified, and (b) that relationship is described to the client when the step is undertaken. When the ultimate treatment goal is to be achieved within a matter of only, say, five to eight sessions, it is easy for clients to see a clear link between a session's accomplishments and the "long-term" goal that is very much in reach because it is only a few more steps and weeks down the road. Under these conditions, energy is mobilized and each step can be understood as meaningful. How is this subgoal by subgoal procession different in brief and longer therapy? Consider this. By the end of the second session of an estimated six session therapy, a client can consider herself/himself to be one-third of the way toward the main treatment goal, that is, almost within its grasp, whereas such a perception is inconceivable after the second session of a 20- to 30-session therapy. This also serves to simplify treatment. Recall that treatment regimen complexity is one of the major determinants of treatment noncompliance (Dunbar & Agras, 1980).

Toward the end of each session, it is useful for the brief therapist to consider what has been done to help the client in that session and identify it. If no obvious helpful step has been taken, the therapist should consider doing something further to help the client. At the very least, the therapist can identify a link between the work of a session and the treatment goals. It is not enough that the therapist perceives progress—this must be shared with and appreciated by the client.

Many of the benefits that occur in brief therapy are also accomplished during early sessions of standard therapy. One difference between the two is that the brief therapist increases the chances of providing assistance by using therapeutic factors in tandem with the abbreviating strategies and by monitoring his or her achievement of short-term goals.

Some readers may wonder if I am advocating that brief therapists simply set small goals, then congratulate themselves for their accomplishment—nothing more than "downsizing," or worse, diminishing treatment aspirations. I do not believe this to be the case. The research reviewed in Chapter Two clearly shows that most of what even long-term therapy accomplishes is attained early in treatment and that therapists (and training texts) often overlook some of the true "active ingredients" of psychotherapy. The strategy I recommend here is designed to understand which activities are most helpful in early sessions so that their presentation can be effectively delivered to all clients, but especially that *majority* who *inevitably* will terminate after a short time in treatment.

THEORY-DERIVED TECHNIQUES

As noted throughout this book, techniques associated with virtually every theoretical orientation have been designed for a brief format and are amply described in brief therapy anthologies (e.g., Bloom, 1992; Wells & Giannetti, 1990; Zeig & Gilligan, 1990). Several micro and macro theoretical orientations are particularly well-suited to a brief format, however, and deserve special mention.

Although psychodynamically oriented therapy in its earlier traditional form (circa 1920 to 1970) is not well-suited to brief therapy, a tremendous amount of work has been successfully devoted to adapting it to brief formats. Several popular approaches to brief dynamic therapy exist; their popularity is such that a professional journal (*International Journal of Brief Therapy*) is devoted to brief dynamic treatment. As noted in Chapter Two, the dynamic approaches are variable with respect to treatment strategies and duration, and provide the briefest of all brief approaches, "single-session" therapy (Bloom, 1992; Talmon, 1990).

One of the great strengths of psychodynamic therapy is that it is based on a broad theory of personality and psychopathology. With respect to the Integrative Model presented earlier, dynamic approaches are therefore conducive to items 3, 4, and 5—conceptualizing, understanding, and predicting as well as exploring the feelings and meanings of problems. Because psychodynamic theory assumes that a relatively few primary themes drive behavior, it is well-suited to the brief therapy task of identifying a thematic focus. And unlike certain other approaches (notably cognitive-behavioral ones), psychodynamic therapies do not require the sequential, specific application of technical procedures that often have prescribed (minimum) numbers of sessions or weeks. In short, dynamic therapies are well-suited to identifying the essence of a person's problems and working on it in a flexible way. Brief therapists of any orientation could benefit by adherence to certain aspects of brief psychodynamic treatment, notably by ensuring that: problems are "named" and explained in a way meaningful to the client, expression of feelings is encouraged, and treatments are applied in a flexible way with respect to problem scope and treatment duration.

Once particular problems are identified, conceptualized, and explored for meaning and feeling, cognitive-behavioral approaches are very useful for problem solving and attaining behavior change. Many of these techniques are very "portable," that is, they can be applied to individual circumscribed problems within a narrow focal issue. Cognitive-behavioral texts are typically organized by target problems and/or treatment techniques so it is possible to use them in a cookbook-style application to brief therapy foci. One word of caution in this regard, however: effective application of cognitive-behavioral techniques requires more than cursory reading about them or attendance at a single training workshop. They are not as simple to use as they may appear in texts. A grounding in the theory behind the technique is needed in order to provide the proper rationale for the client and to cope with the inevitable complications that arise when real (rather than textbook) clients are treated. For the same reasons, clinical supervision by a trained cognitive-behaviorist is required when these techniques are initially applied by a therapist who has not had thorough training and supervision in them. As noted earlier, the reader should be aware that cognitive-behavioral treatment approaches are not necessarily brief, since their commonly prescribed application to multiple or broad foci entails a scope of treatment that is broader than can be accomplished in a brief format. They are easily adapted to brief treatment by applying them to narrow foci.

Strategic psychotherapies and their predecessors (e.g., Bateson, 1979; De Shazer, 1985; Erickson, 1967; Haley, 1973; Watzlawick, Weakland, & Fisch, 1974) are distinguished by an emphasis on client change and problem solving (Rosenbaum, 1990). They usually are described as brief and often employ strategies and techniques that can be used by therapists with a wide range of theoretical orientations. In addition to a general orientation to change, several techniques, such as those described by De Shazer (1985), are described that can be employed cookbook-style to clients. A major advantage of these techniques is that they are usually described in generic psychotherapy language, making them "user-friendly" to psychotherapists of most orientations. Strategic therapists often conceptualize their approach as an integrationist one, designing their techniques for use by therapists from differing orientations. In this way, they are literally made for adoption by therapists who already have an approach to treatment and wish to abbreviate it. A piecemeal use of strategic techniques is not adequate to abbreviate treatment, however, since "strategic" abbreviation derives from comprehensive use of broad treatment strategies and several treatment techniques.

The foregoing is not intended to be a comprehensive listing of strategies and techniques suitable for brief therapy. Rather, I have identified techniques appropriate for brief treatment that are associated with treatment orientations with which the reader is already familiar. They represent technique resources and demonstrate that a number of familiar strategies for helping people can be used in brief treatment. When doing brief treatment, I recommend that therapists rely primarily on adapting their current treatments. If one desires further brief treatment techniques, consider supplementing these with generically described brief treatments (e.g., Budman & Gurman's [1988] approach and crisis therapies as presented by Slaikeu [1984] for example) and approaches, such as those described in the preceding paragraphs, for which they already have some affinity.

All the treatment strategies described thus far in this section can be used to effectively do brief treatment. But the easiest, and perhaps the most effective, way to do brief treatment is to simply *rely on your current treatment techniques*, and focus your efforts on ways to *narrow the scope* of treatment by using the abbreviating strategies described in Chapters Five through Seven. A summary of ways to adapt psychotherapy techniques to a brief format is presented next.

GENERAL RECOMMENDATIONS FOR APPLYING INTERVENTIONS TO A BRIEF FORMAT

This section identifies general strategies for applying techniques from (almost) any treatment approach to a brief format. The emphasis here is not on new interventions, but on how to adapt the ones you prefer using in time-unlimited treatment to brief therapy. The guidelines presented below incorporate much of what has been previously stated regarding the scope and timing of interventions in brief therapy.

1. Apply techniques to the focal problem, not a person's general functioning.

2. Begin use of a technique in the first or second session. This may entail use of a procedure before one is 100 percent sure that it is the best possible technique. As Wolberg (1980, p. 138) states, "in long-term therapy, a dynamic theme that explains the patient's personality operations and resistance gradually reveals itself through a leisurely study. . . . No such casual indulgence is possible in short-term treatment." Many psychotherapeutic procedures are at worst innocuous, so there is no risk of harm to the client or therapy with the early use of such techniques, and a high probability of benefit. Example: At the end of the first session, the therapist is unsure how to best treat a depressed client. A number of treatment techniques are considered possibilities, including Beck's cognitive therapy, problem-solving, and a Lewinsohn-style (1975) treatment that emphasizes systematic assignment of pleasurable activities. The brief therapist would often assign the client to record pleasurable activities in the following week in order to allow the therapist to begin formal implementation of the pleasurable activity treatment at the next session if appropriate. The assignment itself may be therapeutic, since it may stimulate the client to recall or plan pleasant activities. Furthermore, little would be lost if the Lewinsohn treatment were not done.

Another reason to begin low risk aspects of treatment rapidly is that there is often a time lag between the initiation of a treatment and its impact on the client. Behavioral treatments, for example, often entail the establishment of a baseline period before actual behavior changes are suggested. Gathering baseline information on suspected targets after the first visit allows intervention in the second visit.

3. Use two or more interventions simultaneously rather than sequentially. In the interest of identifying the specific aspect of treatment that helps a client, treatment elements are sometimes

introduced sequentially. This has the benefit of the client and therapist knowing exactly "what works" for a given client's problems so that energy can be devoted to the intervention during a treatment episode and in the future if a problem recurs. Unfortunately, many clients will not remain in treatment long enough for implementation of more than one intervention, so the client and therapist never find out which of several interventions are most effective and the client only benefits from the first intervention presented. For example, an aggressive and non-compliant child could be sequentially treated by first having parents administer a reward program for compliant and non-aggressive behaviors followed by training the parents in the use of Time Out and other punishments. In brief therapy, both procedures might be introduced simultaneously. The use of drugs along with psychotherapy early in treatment rather than taking weeks to assess the impact of either one singly is another example of this strategy, used together for the rationale described above.

A word of caution is in order here. It may often be inadvisable to use two interventions concurrently early in treatment; the use of such a strategy should only be considered under select circumstances. The point here is that it warrants consideration for some cases, especially when there is a high probability that a client will not remain in treatment for the time required to implement two or more interventions sequentially (this obtains for *most* cases).

4. Use "homework" assignments. Recommending or assigning activities outside of sessions hastens the impact of many techniques.

5. Aim interventions at modest, concrete treatment goals. Modest goals are achievable; this motivates both client and therapist to work hard because it offers a high probability of tangible success in a brief time.

Use of short-term goals, and identification of a connection between them and long-term goals, further promotes the sense that things are improving for the client.

6. Use problem solving extensively. While problem solving is traditionally aimed at a client's general problem-solving style and a wide range of problems, the brief therapist would more likely use the procedure to address the client's current problems.

SUMMARY

There are a number of things that psychotherapists can do in order to adapt standard therapy techniques to a brief format. Most of the ones recommended in this chapter do not entail learning a new theory of psychopathology or even new treatment techniques. Instead, reliance on one's *current* techniques and style has been emphasized. *Adaptation of standard treatment approaches follows rather naturally if one adopts the abbreviating strategies described in this text.* Their adaptation to a brief format is further facilitated by use of short-term goals in every session and use of some common sense application strategies.

For those relatively few therapists who wish to invest in learning new approaches to treatment theory and techniques, some guidelines for selecting approaches suitable for brief therapy have been provided. For the majority who have developed an approach with which they are satisfied, a conceptual framework for identifying the common interventions of brief therapy was presented. This allows therapists to identify the strategies they rely upon and provides a checklist which may prompt some remediation of relatively weak areas.

CASE EXAMPLE: TREATMENT IMPLEMENTATION

Preliminary Interventions in Sessions One and Two

In the past two chapters the case of Bob has been used to describe rapid assessment, case conceptualization, focus selection, and goal negotiation as they might occur in the first two sessions. Earlier in this chapter (in the section "Assessment/Treatment Planning vs. Intervention: Treatment in the First Session") it was shown that many therapeutic (that is, symptom-reducing) activities typically occur when these procedures are implemented, and that this indeed happened in the first two sessions with Bob.

Treatment in Session One

The abbreviating procedures of rapid assessment, problem conceptualization, and narrowing of the treatment focus were accomplished in the first session. Much was accomplished *therapeutically* also. Throughout the session, the therapist provided a warm, supportive environment that encouraged the client to express his feelings about the situation. The therapist provided a case conceptualization (as illustrated by Figure 6.1) that helped Bob simplify, understand, and organize the previously disorganized, incoherent view of himself as "falling apart." This did much to depathologize the situation and reassure Bob that he was not "going crazy" or "falling apart," but that he had an understandably high stress response to a combination of several interrelated life problems. The therapist was able to reassure Bob that most people subjected to these circumstances would feel greatly distressed. By identifying several potentially treatable foci, Bob was further reassured that there was realistic hope for improvement within a relatively short time. The therapist helped explain the self-perpetuating nature of Bob's upset by describing the diminishment of problem solving that normally accompanies high stress, but added that he was there to help with future problem solving. In the language of the Integrative Model presented earlier, much was done to name the problem and describe its typical course, explore the feelings and meaning of the situation, and put the problem in perspective through attainment of understanding and rational appraisal; that is, elements 3, 4, and 5 were applied. This was all done in the context of a high level of empathy and acceptance (which contributes to element 2). To achieve optimal impact from the process of Session One, the therapist summarized the nature of Bob's plight, the reasons for his symptoms, and the potential for coping with them toward the end of the session.

These actions did much to reduce the client's distress. He was visibly improved during the session: he was less physically agitated, more coherent, and explicitly stated that he felt better about things as a result of seeing them differently. Nevertheless, Bob was still quite upset and dreaded facing more sleepless nights, irritability with others, arguments with his supervisor, and worry over his career and relationship. It was, of course, the therapist's intent to reduce such problems over the course of treatment. Because of his acute distress, an immediate and direct intervention for these problems was warranted. Recall that the last 20 minutes of the first session were reserved for this purpose. Interventions for those last 20 minutes will now be considered.

Exercise: Crisis Intervention in Session One

Orientation

"Crisis intervention" is used here to denote the interventions applied directly to severe symptoms and designed to have rapid impact. As with the rest of treatment, it is acknowledged that there are a number of potentially appropriate crisis intervention targets, and that those selected by a given therapist will depend partly on that therapist's skills, personality, and theoretical orientation. This is not to say that the choice of treatment target should be completely arbitrary, but simply that there may be more than one appropriate target.

Potential Crisis Intervention Foci

A number of distressing symptoms were causing Bob psychic and physical pain. A "micro-conceptualization" of Bob's most distressing symptoms would be useful at this point in order to identify those most troubling, those most easily treated, and those that exacerbate others ("superordinate" symptoms). Considerations relevant to such a conceptualization of Bob's acute problems (potential targets of crisis intervention) follow.

When asked which symptoms bothered him the most, Bob identified his insomnia, noting that the associated fatigue contributed to his irritability and depression. But the insomnia was clearly not a simple independent problem: Bob went to bed and awoke worrying about his life stressors—work conflicts, the thesis, and relationship commitment. The latter worries seem to be superordinate problems, i.e., their reduction could reduce stress symptoms such as anxiety, insomnia, and irritability. The worrisome thoughts created autonomic arousal which caused sleep disruption. While the thoughts would probably not be changed during the 20 minutes of therapy available for crisis intervention in Session One, some degree of the associated arousal might be. The autonomic arousal component of

Bob's stress symptoms might be easiest to treat in the short run because of the numerous "fast-acting" psychological and medical treatments of anxiety.

Potential Interventions

The reader should now consider what could be done to help Bob get through the next week. When workshop and graduate students are asked to do this for similar client situations, a number of interventions are commonly proposed. They include arousal-reducing strategies such as:

- Use of psychoactive medication.
- Relaxation, hypnosis, meditation or similar inductions and training.
- Behavioral "thought-stopping."
- Sleep-inducing (arousal-reducing) techniques such as drinking an alcoholic beverage before bedtime or vigorous physical exercise during the day.
- Insomnia-coping techniques such as adherence to a firm bedtime schedule, leaving the bedroom after awakening during the night, and use of coping self-statements.
- Modeling of assertive communication to be used with Bob's supervisor as a way to reduce arguing.

This is just a short list of a very wide range of interventions proposed by therapists. Bob's therapist recommended consideration of medication from the on-staff psychiatrist, but Bob preferred to try nonmedical interventions. The therapist then took about ten minutes to induce relaxation using Benson's (1975) technique, which emphasizes cognition and meditation. Because Bob had a favorable response to the induction, the therapist taught Bob how to induce relaxation and under what circumstances this might be beneficial (e.g., whenever feeling high arousal and after awakening during the night). This was presented to Bob as a coping skill that he could use in a wide range of situations. In the last five minutes of that session, the therapist briefly described the nature of sleep-wake cycles and recommended the procedures described earlier as "insomnia-coping techniques."

One of the striking experiences I have had in conducting brief therapy classes and workshops is how readily therapists create treatment interventions for application in the last 20 minutes of the first session, regardless of theoretical orientation, professional training, clinical experience, or previous exposure to brief therapy training. Even though clinical techniques (such as relaxation training, hypnosis, or communication training) are almost always depicted as requiring several sessions in training texts, therapists are very adept at adapting them to use in, essentially, a 20-minute segment of a session—20-minute therapy! Readers who engage in the "crisis intervention" exercise above probably also found themselves quite adept at creating some very brief interventions for Bob. I attribute this to primarily two things. First, the time available for treatment dictates content: therapy technique can be altered dramatically to fit various time frames. And second, real clients, as opposed to textbook examples, *often* require this sort of ad-libbed brief therapy, so therapists are actually quite practiced at these brief adaptations. What they do not practice, and often resent and resist, is the idea of planning an entire course of treatment to be very brief. A proper rationale and strategy is needed to overcome the latter.

Session Two

At the beginning of Session Two, Bob reported a diminished level of symptoms so that further crisis intervention was not needed. His sleep was disrupted only three nights in the past week (rather than nightly) and he was able to return to sleep after 20 to 30 minutes. Bob was advised to continue use of the relaxation and insomnia-coping techniques, that had been reported to be moderately successful. Benson's (1975) relaxation was re-administered by the therapist. Most symptoms persisted, but at a more tolerable level.

As described in Chapter Seven, Session Two was devoted to goal negotiation and the associated detailed assessment of issues related to thesis completion. This information was needed for treatment planning and duration estimation, but the process of goal negotiation and focal assessment was itself therapeutic, as it typically is in brief therapy. During the detailed assessment of Bob's thesis problems and related goal negotiations, the therapist explored and gave vent to Bob's (a) feelings about phenomena related to the thesis (for example, Bob's anxiety when faced with a blank page, pride at being a good student, embarrassment over not making thesis progress, resentment that his fiancé tempted him away from thesis work, and (b) attitudes and strategies regarding the thesis work (for example, Bob's belief that he could not devote enough time to complete the thesis because it was such a large task). This allowed for further (and more accurate) definition of this problem, exploration of related feeling, and gaining perspective and understanding of the problem, that is, many items from the Integrative Model were applied.

This process entailed Bob's voicing a number of illogical beliefs. Because the therapist had a cognitive orientation consistent with the illogical belief identification and disputation approaches described by authors such as Beck (1979) and Ellis (Ellis & Harper, 1975), some of the more obviously illogical ideas expressed by Bob (for example, that all aspects of the thesis had to be perfectly executed in order to pass committee review) were noted, gently disputed, and shown to contribute to perpetuating Bob's problems. (Note that this cognitive therapy was not delivered as it usually is prescribed for standard therapy: there was no attempt to make Bob more logical in general. Irrational thoughts specific to thesis completion were targeted.)

The specific assessment inquiries made by the therapist regarding the nature of Bob's thesis and his resources for completing it were intended as the beginning of a problem-solving process. The problem-solving aspect of this exercise was made explicit by the therapist as Bob revealed resources and potential solutions.

By exploring a number of treatment foci and goals and letting Bob choose his preference, the therapist gave Bob a sense of control over the therapy process (important for someone who felt his life was out of control) and communicated confidence and respect for Bob (important for any client, but especially one with low esteem).

In summary, two distinct but interrelated enterprises were pursued in Bob's first two sessions. The therapist both (a) set the pace for a brief treatment by the assessment, conceptualization, focusing, and goal negotiating procedures he employed, and (b) applied several therapeutic interventions, most of which were intrinsic to the processes in "(a)" or easily integrated with them.

The next therapy task was to get from the identification of the treatment goal to its accomplishment within the time frame allotted (nine to 12 sessions). Clearly, much of what was to be done in the remaining session was influenced by the dense activity of the first two.

Exercise: Create a Treatment Plan for Session Three to Termination

There are a number of ways that treatment might proceed at this point. Before the particular course chosen by Bob's therapist is described, the reader is encouraged to consider how s/he might proceed, assuming that Sessions One and Two occurred as described so far. To summarize: The therapist has identified several interrelated life situations (conflict with his work supervisor, impending work relocation of his fiancé and associated commitment indecision, and inability to complete a Master's thesis, all exacerbated by being out of phase with age peers on career and relationship issues) that have contributed to several somatic and emotional symptoms. The client has identified coping with the thesis as the preferred focus of treatment and has selected submitting a polished draft and scheduling his thesis orals as the treatment goal. Client and therapist agreed that accomplishment of this goal would reduce or eliminate many of Bob's presenting problems. Within the identified time frame of nine to 12 sessions, it may also be feasible to spend time addressing some of the other presenting problems directly, but not in a comprehensive fashion.

Several therapeutic interventions have been applied through the first two sessions, including naming the problem, exploring client feelings, gaining understanding of the problem, and some initial problem-solving. In addition, relaxation training, rational discussion of certain illogical beliefs, and insomnia-coping procedures were applied as a sort of crisis therapy in order to reduce the severity of distress to a tolerable level.

The task at this point is to help Bob reach his goal of completing his thesis and achieve the presumed associated improvements in adjustment. This entails the creation of a treatment plan. During the second session, the details of Bob's thesis and time schedule revealed (somewhat misleadingly) a simple strategy: complete one of the six components of the thesis each week (recall that there were six steps involved in his thesis, each of which required about ten to 14 hours, and that Bob had about 15 hours of time to devote to the thesis each week). Bob was a very bright, competent student who had been highly motivated to do his thesis, but was still unable to do so, however. He claimed that his "mind went blank" and he became extremely anxious and unable to produce quality work when attempting to work on his thesis. Bob also had a history of procrastination and anxiety with other complex academic tasks, so a "just do it" strategy would not be adequate—the task of therapy would be to overcome Bob's inability to do thesis work despite his earnest efforts.

In many ways, the focus and goal selected set the agenda and structure for the rest of Bob's treatment. They dictated that the basic strategy would be to try to find and then overcome the obstacles to thesis completion. Therapy therefore became the further understanding of and coping with Bob's thesis creation process. Therapists who are highly experienced with problems similar to Bob's (e.g., procrastination, performance anxieties, and paralyzing fears) probably could readily formulate a relevant treatment plan for Bob at this point.

The reasoning used by Bob's therapist in creating a treatment plan will be made explicit in order to illustrate how this occurs in brief therapy. The first step was to identify the obstacles to thesis completion. Depending on one's theoretical orientation, these might be conceptualized as intrapsychic, attitudinal, relational, or environmental.

Bob's anxiety when doing thesis work seemed a central component of his problem; his report that his mind went blank was an obvious obstacle to the thesis. Because the anxious state is aversive, he was motivated to avoid or escape thesis work; the recreational activities provided by his fiancé functioned as an escape and were problematic. (Indeed, aspects of the relationship could have conceptual and treatment priority with some therapists.) A number of attitudes and beliefs contributed to Bob's anxiety. He was very demanding of his academic output—he overly criticized his own work. He also became overwhelmed by the size of the thesis task: he focused on the size of the total task and found the relatively small number of hours available each as grossly inadequate to address the total task. His normal routine was to sit down to do his work, immediately get anxious, struggle to produce a small amount of work, judge that work as inadequate, feel pressure to produce more and better work, get more anxious, and then have even greater difficulty doing his work.

It was straightforward to identify cognitive and behavioral interventions to address this formulation. Such interventions could include: anxiety-reducing techniques such as relaxation training and systematic desensitization; cognitive treatments for identifying and replacing anxiety-producing ideas; and environmental control such as finding a place where work will not be interrupted. Therapists from other theoretical orientations might emphasize discussions of earlier (including childhood) achievement experiences; communication training and discussion of relationship issues regarding the fiancé or supervisor (as long as such approaches maintained a focus on how these relationships contribute to Bob's thesis anxiety); or fantasizing about successful future thesis work as a means to generate solutions to the thesis impasse. In addition to interfering with Bob's thesis work itself, Bob's anxiety seemed to have impaired his problem-solving abilities for doing the thesis (e.g., creating a thesis work schedule and identification of work locations). So assistance in problem solving was an important consideration.

All the treatment techniques considered in this section are drawn from the standard therapy tradition—none were created for brief therapy. I am confident that most readers found it fairly easy to identify treatment techniques to be used with Bob regardless of the reader's theoretical orientation. What makes these standard techniques adaptable to brief therapy for Bob are the application of strategies identified earlier in this chapter, that is, application of treatment to the focal problem, use of treatment in the first session, identification of short-term goals for each session, and so on.

Treatment Summary for the Case Example

A realistic depiction of a course of treatment for Bob is summarized below. Sessions One and Two are only very briefly summarized here because of their elaborate previous portrayal.

Sessions One and Two Summary

Most of the "pre-intervention" foundations of treatment abbreviation were accomplished in these sessions, including assessment, creation and sharing of a case conceptualization, establishment of a treatment focus and goals, and estimation of treatment duration. In the course of so doing, common treatment elements such as naming the problem, exploring feelings, and developing a therapeutic relationship were provided. Crisis intervention was used to lower stress and improve sleep.

Session Three

At the beginning of the session, Bob announced he was hopeful that he was on the right track regarding his problems, and that his general stress level had further diminished. He only had two nights with sleep disruption but continued to argue with his boss. The main improvement was outside of work: he had fewer worries about his career and relationship. Treatment emphasized the following:

(a) An inspection of Bob's thesis materials and a discussion of his review of them. This confirmed the earlier estimation that the thesis was composed of six parts, each of which entailed 15 to 20 hours of work.

(b) Strategies were devised to prevent Bob's flight into recreation when thesis work was attempted. This entailed scheduling thesis work during times that his fiancé was at work and going to the local public library.

(c) Bob and the therapist reviewed how Bob was to present this thesis work schedule to his fiancé. Bob appeared confident and competent to do this assertively without creating conflict.

(d) Bob elaborated his perceptions of the thesis task as he sat down to work on it: he repeatedly thought about the great amount of effort needed to complete the thesis and the little time available to do it each week. The therapist redefined the thesis task as only the part of it assigned for that week. Bob had frequent irrational thoughts in this regard, such as "I'll never finish this," "I'll do lousy work," "I shouldn't have to give up my weekends for the thesis," and "I'll be miserable without any free time." Bob presented these ideas with conviction and a neurotic, hopeless style.

Cognitive therapy adapted from Beck et al. (1979) and Ellis (Ellis & Harper, 1985) was used along with Rogerian (Rogers, 1951) style support in order to cope with these thoughts. Rather than use the standard therapy technique of having a client record all emotional upsets and related thoughts (cf., Ellis & Harper, 1975), the therapist wrote down logical alternatives to the four illogical thoughts (cited above) that Bob said occurred most often when he tried to work on his thesis. Further rational discussion/cognitive therapy was planned for the next session. Bob was instructed to use the Benson relaxation procedure and rational thought to cope with anxiety when doing thesis work.

(e) Bob expressed guilt and fear over the possibilities of failure in his relationship. Rogerian-style expression of empathy and acceptance were employed to deal with this, but the topic of the thesis completion was reintroduced by the therapist after Bob's bad feelings diminished and he identified a friend with whom he could further discuss this issue.

Out-of-session work: The therapist asked Bob to attempt to do just one-half of the first part of the thesis using the work times, locations, and strategies they had worked out. The therapist used a paradoxical communication in this regard. He told Bob that the purpose of this was *not* to complete the thesis work, but to simply further assess his thoughts and feelings and the impact of the coping strategies (relaxation, logical self-statements, thesis-work setting, communications with fiancé) they had devised.

Session Four

Bob reported having the same moderated stress level and insomnia as the previous week. He also said that he worked for 12 hours and completed the first (one-sixth) part of his thesis. He was pleased with this but cautious, noting that he completed the easiest part of the thesis. Most of the session was devoted to discussion of Bob's attitude and beliefs about the thesis as identified in Session Three. Bob acknowledged the illogic of some (but not all) and acknowledged that *all* such thoughts interfered with thesis work, upset him, and would be better substituted by rational alternatives. More rational alternatives were discussed. Afterward, Bob wrote down those alternative thoughts that he considered helpful for use during thesis work. He reported being reassured by the cognitive therapy discussions in-session.

Bob reported that he felt more self-accepting of his ambivalence about his relationship with his fiancé, and that he was reassured further by discussing this with a trusted friend. Treatment duration was addressed in light of the first four sessions. It was estimated that three to four more sessions would be needed to help Bob through all six parts of the thesis, plus another session or two to help cope with feedback/corrections and anxiety about the oral examination. These estimates were based on anticipation that the supervisor conflicts, relationship commitment, or Bob's other life problems would at some point have to be dealt with to some degree in order to maintain Bob's emotional equilibrium.

After Bob volunteered that he had his best sleep in months after playing racquetball one day in the past week, the therapist noted the potential stress-reducing effect of exercise. Bob also revealed how upset he was over his recent weight gain and how out of control this made him feel. An impromptu exercise/weight loss plan was discussed as a possibility: Bob identified some mild exercise activities he would try (three days a week, 20 minutes each), and the therapist calculated the calorie intake that would yield a one- to two-pound weight loss per week for Bob (the therapist had a background in health psychology). The therapist and Bob agreed that not enough therapy time was available for the therapist to direct Bob's weight control efforts. He could provide some minimal consulting but most of this program would have to be created by Bob himself or with the assistance of a reputable program such as the local Weight Watchers. The therapist lent Bob a calorie book and recommended he count calories for a couple of days if he decided to pursue weight loss.

Work conflict continued but time for addressing it was unavailable. This was to be addressed if time became available in future sessions.

Out-of-session work: Bob was urged to undertake the second part of the thesis, using the strategies applied in the previous week, augmented by the additional rational self-statements generated during this session. The exercise program devised in the session was written into Bob's calendar-style datebook. He was cautioned to undertake the weight control only if he had sufficient time and energy for it–the thesis was the priority.

Session Five

Bob reported that his distress was significantly reduced outside of the work setting: sleep patterns and mood were nearly normal. He continued to have upsetting frequent conflicts with his supervisor at work. He worked for 12 of the scheduled 18 thesis hours and completed about three-quarters of the assigned task. His schedule was interrupted by an out-of-town guest's visit but he was confident that he was learning to cope effectively with the thesis.

Bob counted calories for three days and, using a formula provided by the therapist, estimated the amount of food he could consume daily in order to achieve modest weight loss. Bob appeared quite enthused about the exercise/weight loss program and reported exercising four (rather that the self-assigned three) times last week. The therapist gave some advice for improving some aspects of the weight loss and exercise programs.

Given that Bob failed to do all his thesis work, much of the session reviewed ways to cope with anxiety, work schedule, and other potential interruptions of the thesis. Bob fully accepted the rationale for disputing illogical thoughts and reported this primarily enabled him to reduce anxiety when doing thesis work. He attributed sleep improvement to his exercise program.

Since other matters were going fairly well, the supervisor conflicts were addressed in the last ten minutes of the session. Bob expressed much anger and had difficulty considering assertive options to his aggressive communications.

Out-of-session work: Bob was assigned to complete his work from the previous week and try to complete part three of the thesis. He was also asked to monitor his conversations with his work supervisor and report on them in the next session.

Session Six

Bob was pleased to report a very productive week regarding thesis work: he completed the previous week's (incomplete) task,

Session Five's assignment for the thesis (the second of the six thesis components), and the following component of the thesis. Three of the six parts of the thesis—half of it—were now completed. It appeared that Bob had mastered the thesis work and was well on his way to completing it.

Bob also kept up his exercise and weight loss routine, and had joined the local Weight Watchers. He had lost three pounds in the past two weeks.

Bob reported that his mood and sleep had been normal for the past week except for some upsets on the job. The attainment of near normal mood and apparent mastery of the thesis problem allowed more thorough assessment of Bob's other issues, the supervisor conflict and commitment issue. (The therapist made a clinical judgment to inquire about these other issues based on their earlier contribution to Bob's upsets. One could argue that this decision should have been negotiated with Bob rather than a unilateral decision by the therapist. That is, the therapist could have offered Bob the alternative of terminating this session early or pursuing the other issues.)

Despite the progress with thesis and weight loss/exercise, Bob expressed concern over continued conflicts with his supervisor: they had a heated argument in the past week that apparently upset both of them. Since Bob now felt confident that he would finish his thesis, the prospect of quitting this job and finding another interim job was discussed. Bob decided to stay with the job, claiming he "could handle the conflict" even though it was clearly upsetting to him. In longer-term treatment, this issue probably would have been the subject of several sessions. The therapist asked Bob if he were interested in devoting three to six sessions (beyond the number originally estimated for the entire course of treatment) to this issue, but Bob declined. Importantly, Bob said that his conflicts on the job did not upset him enough to impact his sleep or relationship.

Bob also acknowledged some continued ambivalence about commitment to his fiancé. Bob claimed that the relationship was going as well as it ever had, and that the commitment issue was something he wanted to work out on his own and in discussions with friends. He reported that the issue caused him little distress, and, indeed, he seemed comfortable with it.

Bob appeared quite competent to continue work on the thesis with little assistance. He felt that the other issues were sufficiently under control to warrant scheduling the next session in two weeks.

Session Seven

Bob continued progress toward thesis completion: two more sections were completed (making 5 of 6 completed). He felt very good about this and noted continued good general adjustment: normal affect, sleep, and relations with others except for his supervisor. There were no major arguments at work, relations with his fiancé were normal, and he had lost an additional four pounds. Bob was very pleased with treatment even though the supervisor conflicts and relationship ambivalence remained. He considered these within the bounds of normal life difficulties. Session Eight was scheduled in two weeks. He was to have completed the thesis, begun revising and "polishing" it, and submitted a draft to his advisor.

Session Eight

Bob had submitted a draft of his thesis to his advisor and had been given permission to schedule his oral defense. It was scheduled four weeks hence.

Adjustment continued to be normal, even though Bob had made a major change: he had quit his job and taken another that was three-quarters time. He was very pleased with this, and looked forward to using his free time for applying for jobs.

Bob expressed some growing anxiety about performing poorly during his oral defense. Discussion revealed that this fear was linked to worry over poor preparation. Rehearsal of the orals with classmates was identified as a means of coping with this concern. Self-induced relaxation and coping self-statements, used previously in early sessions, were reviewed as additional means of coping.

Therapy goals were reviewed. Bob felt that they had been reached and, more importantly, he had attained a normal level of adjustment. Bob said he was happy with his adjustment and felt able to cope with the remaining issues, which he regarded as normal problems in living.

A final one-half hour session was scheduled in three and a half weeks (four days before the oral defense) in order to support Bob and review his adjustment.

Session Nine

Bob appeared very confident with his readiness for his oral defense. He was also pleased with his new job and that he had lost a total of ten pounds during therapy. Mood and sleep remained normal. While still not sure of his commitment to his fiancé, he was far more comfortable with the prospects of either remaining in or breaking off the relationship.

Consistent with the previously agreed upon treatment goals, treatment was terminated.

Treatment Summary

Although not all of Bob's problems were thoroughly addressed, significant improvement was achieved. Bob attained a level of adjustment consistent with that of most of his adult life, one that was very acceptable to him and absent any diagnosable or severe psychopathology. His original presenting problems—a mid-life crisis with symptoms of depression, anxiety, sleep loss, appetite disturbance, irritability, and a subjective sense of helplessness—were eliminated or diminished to an acceptable level. Certain problems did remain: Bob never did (during therapy) come to a decision about commitment to his fiancé or deal with the general issue of commitment; he never learned to communicate assertively with his supervisor; and his general procrastinating style was not addressed.

It is easy to see how a shorter or longer treatment might have proceeded with Bob. A longer treatment could have addressed some or all of the remaining problems. A shorter therapy could be defended also: by Session Six, the focal thesis issue was well on its way to being solved with consequent improvement in overall adjustment. It seems that a radical three-session therapy would have been much better than no therapy at all—it is clear that many symptoms significantly diminished and Bob was able to begin his thesis before the fourth session.

This therapy is obviously not reducible to a simple matter of helping someone do a thesis. The thesis, rather, was the focal point for addressing some of the broader issues connected to it and affected by it.

Chapter Nine

Importance of the First Two Sessions

Chapters Five through Seven illustrate that most of the critical techniques and strategies of treatment abbreviation—rapid assessment and case conceptualization, focus identification, and goal establishment—are typically accomplished during the first two sessions of brief therapy. The last chapter (eight) showed that important *treatment*, that is, direct assistance for the client, also occurs in those initial sessions. Research that has examined the degree of clinical improvement associated with different stages of therapy provides empirical support for this latter assertion. As reviewed in Chapter Two, several studies have found that there is substantial improvement associated with one to two sessions of therapy; this is supported by experimental studies of random assignment to one to two sessions vs. time-unlimited treatment (e.g., Edwards et al., 1977; Miller & Hester, 1986) as well as a much larger number of studies that have addressed improvement at different stages of therapy (e.g., Howard et al., 1986; Howard et al., 1993; Gottschalk, Mayerson, & Gottlieb, 1967; Pekarik, 1983a). Howard et al.'s 1993 work illustrates the improvement associated with the initial two sessions very clearly. Figure 9.1 shows the amount of improvement achieved on three different outcome measures at the second, fourth, and seventeenth sessions.

This figure shows why the authors concluded that there was a dramatic change in subjective well-being by the second session. The majority of improvement achieved during the entire 17 sessions had occurred by the second session for all three measures! Obviously, the first sessions of all psychotherapy are important, and this is especially true of brief therapy.

When assessment, case conceptualization, focus identification,

Figure 9.1. Mean *T* scores for subjective well-being, symptomatic distress (reversed), and current life functioning for selected sessions of psychotherapy.

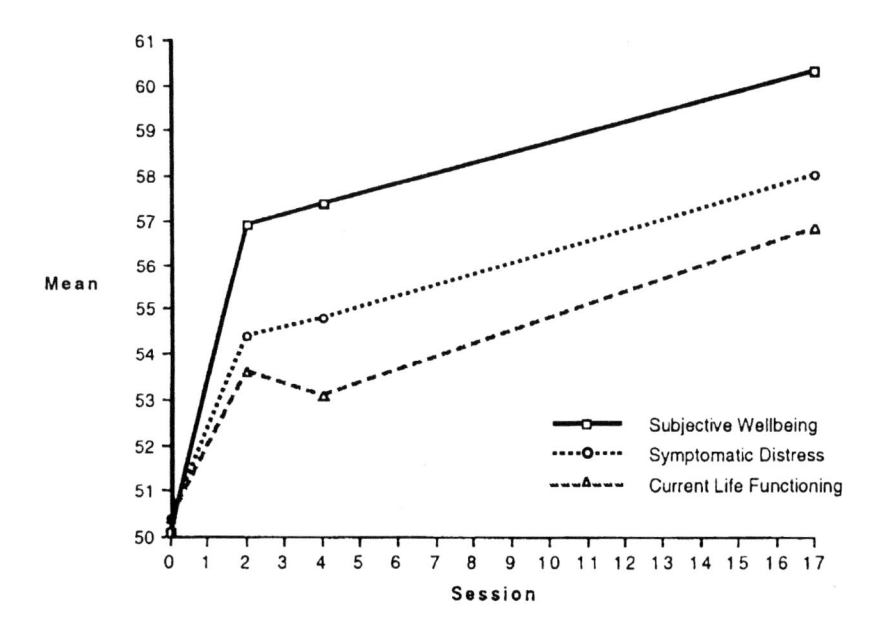

(From "A Phase Model of Psychotherapy Outcome: Causal Mediation of Change" by K. I. Howard, R. L. Lueger, M. S. Maling, and Z. Martinovich, 1993, *Journal of Consulting and Clinical Psychology, 61,* 678-685. Copyright 1993 by the American Psychological Association. Reprinted by permission.)

and goal negotiation are all accomplished in the first sessions, much of the rest of therapy has been determined. Both client and therapist know what will be addressed (focus), why the focal problem exists (conceptualization), what type and degree of changes will be pursued (goals), and about how long it will take to attain these changes (duration). Moreover, much of the character of treatment is also established as a result of such early session activity: Often the therapist communicates the basic structure of sessions, that there will be continuity across sessions by continued emphasis on the focal issue, that a level of accountability will be attained by monitoring progress toward goals, and that therapy-related activity outside of the sessions will be expected. By the end of the second session, a treatment plan has also been identified (or is being prepared by the therapist). With this much in place, the remainder of treatment primarily consists of following through on these earlier actions. This involves treating the chosen focal issue and making mid-course corrections based on information that emerges during the treatment process.

Considerable skill is required to accomplish the treatment follow-through during the remainder of a treatment course, but, as was shown in the previous chapter, the technical skills for doing this are possessed by most therapists with or without special training in brief therapy. The major pitfall is the tendency to digress into nonfocal issues and disparage what can be accomplished in a short time. If the brief therapist accepts a rationale for brief therapy and pursues the agreed-upon goals within the focal area, such digressions can be avoided. Under these circumstances, the abbreviation of treatment is a normal and natural process.

The converse of the above is also true: if the therapist conducts the first therapy sessions as s/he would with standard or time-unlimited therapy, it is very difficult to orient treatment to a brief approach at a later time. It is not a good idea to begin treatment with a standard approach with the hope of shifting to a time-sensitive approach later. This results in confusion and sometimes resentment by clients who are asked to change from a broadly focused, slow pace to a narrowly focused, faster one.

Many brief therapists have commented on the importance of the first brief therapy sessions. Budman et al. (1992) have even edited a book on "The First Session in Brief Therapy." Because of the importance of the first two sessions of brief therapy, the rest of this brief chapter is devoted to an outline of the tasks to accomplish in those sessions. The outline summarizes most of the abbreviating and early intervention techniques described in Chapters Five through Eight, with an emphasis in procedures unique to brief therapy, that is, those that most perpetuate time-sensitivity. This outline represents a concise "manual" of the procedures to use for treatment abbreviation.

TASKS TO ACCOMPLISH: SESSION ONE

1. Identify treatment focus using brief assessment.
   (a) Identify the presenting problem.
   (b) Describe what the client *does* that defines the problem.
   (c) Two key questions: Why did the client enter treatment at this particular time? What needs to be accomplished so that the client would feel no further need of treatment?
   (d) Consider the following foci hierarchy: simple, circumscribed problem; crisis; behavioral or emotional symptoms; personality.
2. Negotiate the long-term goal with the client.
   (a) Find out what the client hopes to get out of treatment.
   (b) Define the goal as an achievement, not a process.
   (c) Define in terms that are clear, specific, and verifiable.
   (d) Estimate length of treatment needed for two alternative prospective goals.
3. Do something that will help the client *today*.
   (a) Provide empathic listening.
   (b) Provide a case conceptualization.
   (c) If appropriate, take direct steps to provide immediate problem or symptom relief in the session. Consider:
      i) psychotherapeutic techniques such as relaxation training, advice-giving, and "de-pathologizing" certain acts, feelings, etc.
      ii) immediate problem solving, such as telephoning a consultant or making an appointment with a professional or agency.
   (d) Consider a homework assignment that is either therapeutic in itself or facilitates an anticipated intervention in Session Two.
4. Consider a treatment plan for the course of treatment.
   (a) If enough information is now available, identify the treatment plan.
   (b) If enough information is not available to identify a treatment plan, identify the questions that must be asked to secure the needed information.
   (c) Is there a "state of the art" brief treatment available for your client's problem?

5. Plan your agenda for the next session.
   (a) Consider what can be done to help the client next week.
   (b) What will you do next week that will continue (or start) the treatment plan?

TASKS TO ACCOMPLISH: SESSION TWO

1. Review the work of the previous session for the client (focus, conceptualization, and goals) i.e., orient client to the current stage of the treatment process.
2. If "Tasks of Session One" were not done, pick up where you left off on that outline.
3. Review homework or outside consultation.
4. Initiate the treatment plan (if not previously initiated) or implement the next stage of the plan.
5. Make sure that today's treatment does something to help the client now (if this is difficult, at least do #6 below).
6. Review the current session and indicate how it fits in with the treatment plan.
7. Assign outside of session activity if appropriate.

TASKS TO ACCOMPLISH: SESSIONS THREE THROUGH TERMINATION

1. Review the previous session or otherwise orient client to the current stage of treatment.
2. Review relevant outside of session activity.
3. Continue the treatment process according to plan (digress only to cope with a crises or significant new development).
4. Try to do something that is helpful today; at least do #6 below.
5. Assign the outside of session activity if appropriate.
6. Review the session and indicate how it fits in with the treatment plan.

These six steps can be summarized as "review, treat, help, assign, review."

Chapter Ten

Issues in the Practice of Brief Therapy

In this book I have tried to show that there are sound humanitarian and pragmatic reasons for enthusiastically using brief therapy with many clients–in many ways, it is the best treatment for many clients. I have also shown that most therapists, with relatively little training, can become adept at doing brief therapy if they have the proper motivation to do so. Despite this, there is resistance and resentment against brief therapy by many therapists. Much of this is the result of the conditions under which therapists often do brief therapy: uniform (across cases) and arbitrary reimbursement restrictions by third-party payers, usually under the name of managed care, that coerce therapists to do brief treatment. There is considerably more to this story than simple managed care (i.e., autonomy incursion) resentments, however, for the managing of mental health care and associated forced treatment abbreviation occurs in a context wherein the time-unlimited treatment model has greatly influenced therapist values and treatment delivery policies. It is difficult to practice brief therapy under the circumstances of historical aggrandizement of long-term therapy and forced conduct of abbreviated treatment.

One hundred years of predominantly time-unlimited psychotherapy has created practices, attitudes, and a subculture that are often incompatible with the conduct of brief therapy. Certain changes in training, practice, and administrative policies could facilitate the effective delivery of brief therapy and the professional satisfaction of those who do it. This chapter will review traditional resistance and practical obstacles to brief therapy; identify potential advantages of doing brief therapy for the therapist; and recommend organization, administrative policy, and training changes that would facilitate the conduct of effective brief therapy.

THE PSYCHOTHERAPIST SUBCULTURAL CONTEXT: RESISTANCE TO BRIEF THERAPY

Idealization of Long-Term Treatment

Many authors have noted that historically there has been a clear value for long-term therapy among psychotherapists (e.g., Bloom, 1984, 1992; Gelso & Johnson, 1983; Karasu, 1987; O'Hanlon & Weiner-Davis, 1989). Bloom (1992, pg. 5) has succinctly summarized this attitude: "brief treatment is thought of as superficial, longer is equated with better, and the most influential and prestigious practitioners tend to be those who undertake intensive long-term therapy with a very limited number of clients."

Therapists are introduced to this value system early in their training, where texts and case presentations emphasize longer-term treatment. As elaborately documented in Chapter Two, even *brief* therapy texts emphasize treatments toward the longer end of that approach, that is, 15 to 20 sessions, even though brief therapy authors are more aware than anyone that most clients terminate by the tenth session. The preference for longer treatment is associated with several myths and misconceptions about brief therapy.

Negative Beliefs About Brief Therapy

There are a number of negative stereotypes about brief therapy held by many therapists. While some of these may be somewhat valid, a good number are not. Baldwin (1977, 1979) has identified a number of "myths and misconceptions" about crisis intervention that capture many of the negative beliefs about brief therapy. Among them he cites beliefs that brief intervention: is only appropriate for emergencies; demands less skill and training than standard therapy; represents a stop-gap action until longer treatment can be provided; and does not produce lasting change. The most serious reservation held about brief therapy is its "superficiality" and inferiority to longer treatment. Some therapists believe that certain critical aspects of psychotherapy cannot be effectively executed in a brief time; more generally, many believe that if some therapy is good, more is better (Hoyt, 1985). Although these contentions have been basically refuted by research cited throughout this book, especially in Chapter Two, they are still held by many therapists.

Practical Advantages of Long Therapy

A powerful incentive to extend treatment duration is a financial one. For private practitioners, each session represents substantial income; each reduction in treatment duration represents a loss of income. In an increasingly competitive service-delivery market, this is a serious economic issue. In addition, each time a case is opened and closed, additional administrative tasks (e.g., completing insurance forms and intake and closing summaries; making phone calls to set up appointments) are required that are not reimbursed and are inherently onerous. (It is interesting to note that while there has been a virtual explosion of interest in ethical problems associated with curtailing treatment by managed care, the ethical problem of inducing unnecessary treatment is almost never addressed by mental health professionals.)

There are also important experiential incentives to extending treatment. Early sessions are inherently stressful to therapists. The goodness of fit between client and therapist is unknown at the first session and often problematic: the base rate of client rejection of treatment is high and occurs most often in early sessions (about 30 percent terminate in the first two sessions). Each additional session with a known client avoids the risky encounter with a new client. The obverse of this issue is that clients who have attended several sessions have moved past the risky early sessions and have demonstrated their commitment to and satisfaction with the therapeutic relationship. They thus provide both financial and experiential rewards to the therapist with each visit. The intense work of the brief therapist is undoubtedly more stressful than the comparatively relaxed encounters between "old friends" that evolve in longer therapy. Many brief therapists have commented on this inherent advantage of longer treatment (Bloom, 1992; Budman & Gurman, 1988; Carmona, 1988; Hoyt, 1985).

Advantages Inherent in Brief Therapy

The research literature on brief therapy reviewed in Chapter Two identified several findings that suggest some distinct advantages for the therapist who conducts brief therapy. The low dropout rate, early session improvement, and high client satisfaction associated with brief therapy should contribute to a brief therapist's job satisfaction. In earlier chapters it was also shown that brief therapy embodies many of the treatment preferences and expectations of clients, for example, to target modest goals and be cost-effective. The brief therapist who is aware of these compatibilities and aligns with clients' pursuit of these preferences may find enhanced work satisfaction as a result. Simply knowing that one is providing clients with the high quality efficient treatment they desire can be very gratifying.

Beyond these empirically demonstrated positive elements of brief therapy, there is also the issue of therapy style. Unlike the traditional therapist, the brief therapist is not required to doggedly pursue a theory-defined state of optimal functioning, to fix everything, to "cure" a client. These ambitious strivings, which are usually at odds with client preferences and attendance patterns, can be a source of great frustration for therapists and can make treatment an almost adversarial relationship at times. In brief therapy, the therapist is given permission to accept the more limited presenting problem as a legitimate treatment target. It can be a very liberating experience for a therapist to pursue issues that the client is highly motivated to address and to terminate treatment before a point of diminishing returns is met.

Because the biggest improvements usually occur early in treatment, the brief therapist gets to witness a lot of dramatic client gains and high client turnover introduces the brief therapist to a more varied caseload. Brief therapy, then, is especially compatible with therapists who enjoy challenges and observing major clinical gains in a short time, and can tolerate the higher rate of difficult (i.e., new) clients. While this characterization correctly suggests that brief therapy is more stressful than standard treatment for the therapist, this is partly offset by the reduced pressure to achieve clinical perfection, that is, to eliminate all dysfunction. This reduced pressure is achieved only if one has the proper attitude toward brief therapy (as described throughout this book, but especially in Chapter Four), so it is very important for brief therapists to work on this. Each individual therapist must address this attitude in order to function happily as a brief therapist. In addition to the individual's efforts, there are certain administrative/organizational policies that can also help cope with the particular stressors associated with doing brief therapy.

Administrative/Organizational Issues

The nature of service delivery systems can affect the conduct of brief therapy. As already noted, fee-for-service arrangements often greatly discourage treatment abbreviation by financial penalty. A policy of 100 percent reimbursement for the first few sessions followed by increasing co-payments for greater sessions would greatly increase treatment access (Giannetti, 1990). In the same way, it has been noted that reimbursement of "first dollar" costs rather than higher, later costs has the effect of preventing mild problems from worsening by increasing intervention access at an early problem stage (Kiesler & Morton, 1988). A study at a managed care clinic illustrates the power of co-payment policies: 100 percent reimbursement (i.e., "free" service) for the first three sessions followed by a 50 percent co-payment resulted in 88 percent of clients terminating treatment by the fifth session (Pekarik, 1992). The particular ways that costs are managed affect the mental health of client and therapist. Currently, a common insurance company practice is to increase co-payments with increased sessions, effectively eliminating treatment for most people after a 50 to 80 percent co-payment is reached, usually by about 12 to 15 sessions. Similarly, some programs limit outpatient treatment to a fixed low number of sessions. Such policies are neither logical nor humanitarian, since some clients obviously warrant more treatment than others. A more enlightened approach to controlling costs is to assign an average number of sessions for a clinic or therapist's caseload so that the therapist has flexibility to provide sessions based on need. Another acceptable approach would be to set a target number of sessions for certain clinical problems, subject to increased sessions contingent on a "continued stay review" (see further discussion of these options in Chapter Three). Restricting sessions to an arbitrary fixed number unnecessarily elicits resentment from both clients and therapists. The proper training of a brief therapy rationale, along with treatment that allowed clients to follow their normal preferences for brief treatment, would by itself reduce treatment costs. Only moderate and flexible outpatient session controls are needed for cost control under such circumstances (assuming control of more costly inpatient treatment).

Even without the financial incentives to do longer treatment, clinicians are inclined toward longer treatment. Pekarik & Finney-Owen (1987) found a clear preference for longer treatment even among salaried public clinic clinicians. The experiential advantages of long-term treatment, organizational policies inherited from a long-term treatment model, and a subculture and history that lauds longer treatment all discourage the use of brief therapy. Organizational policy changes could do much to reverse this, so that brief therapy is less stressful and more rewarding to practitioners.

Steps can be taken to reduce the stress associated with the increased work intensity of brief therapy. Use of more frequent breaks and scheduling of fewer clients is one obvious solution. Because the high turnover of clients exposes brief therapists to more clients and more (ethically and legally) risky situations, this should be addressed by such means as structured therapist peer support group meetings and consultation, group supervision, continuing education, and case conference presentations. While such actions that reduce client contact have some associated costs, these could be offset by improved therapist morale, effectiveness, and efficiency. It should be kept in mind that, when working under a capitated contract, efficient brief therapists save money for the employer-contractor (even if the "employer" is a therapist's own practice, as is the case when a practice or practice consortium owns the contract), so it makes economic sense to reward cost-effective therapists. The kind of therapist-supportive procedures described here are designed to reward the conduct of brief therapy and maintain therapist effectiveness and efficiency in the long run. Overloading any therapist, and especially a brief therapist, is a prescription for therapist burnout, resulting in lowered efficiency, effectiveness, and morale (Maslach, 1978). While therapist overwork can make profits in the *short run*, an organization's reputation for good work is associated with *keeping* contracts. Psychotherapists are similar to athletes in this regard—the best long-term performance is achieved by moderate to high activity (i.e., doing therapy), a good conditioning program (e.g., peer group meetings), and good coaching (access to consultation and supervision).

Under other than fee-for-service arrangements (e.g., HMOs, some public clinic clients), it is also feasible and logical to consider giving therapists financial rewards for efficient and effective work. I suggest this with some reluctance and caution, for it could undermine both quality of work and therapist mental health if not done properly. The proper use of incentives would consider efficiency (e.g., average number of sessions), caseload difficulty (e.g., client diagnosis and other characteristics), and, importantly, quality of care. Quality of care here depends on systematic, methodologically sound means of assessing *both* outcome and satisfaction (which are virtually independent of one another). Yates (1994) has described procedures for assessing treatment cost-effectiveness that could be used in this regard. (Further discussion of outcome issues is discussed in a later section on training and research.) Hoffman and Remmel (1975) have proposed that higher hourly fees be charged to brief therapy cases since the total cost of a course of treatment is reduced by brief therapy; they report successful use of this strategy in a family service agency. Carefully implemented, this seems to be a promising way to reward brief therapists for their more intensive work, either by giving them a higher salary or reducing their required billable hours.

A reduction in treatment-related paperwork would be a simple but effective way to facilitate brief therapy. Great amounts of thankless paperwork tasks accumulate when standard forms are used to track clients in brief therapy; each bit of paperwork is a punishment for treatment abbreviation, since intake and termination paperwork is in direct proportion to treatment brevity. Settings that wish to abbreviate treatment should seriously address this problem by eliminating unnecessary paperwork and making what remains as easy as possible. Forms with checklists and blank spaces to fill in, for example, are much easier to do than those with open-ended questions. Assigning as much of the paperwork as possible to office staff would be a cost-effective way to use staff time as well as increase therapist morale.

TRAINING AND PROFESSIONAL DEVELOPMENT ISSUES

Research on Training in Brief Therapy

The mental health field is in the midst of a dramatic change in the way services are delivered. Cummings (1995) has likened this to the industrial revolution of the 1800s, noting that both the means of service delivery and the content of psychotherapy has changed, with managed care and brief therapy dominating. These changes have occurred rapidly. As recently as 1992 managed care was perceived by many as a temporary aberration (Wright, 1992). Previous to the 1990s, brief therapy was an interest of a minority of practitioners. Although many claim to practice brief therapy to some degree, most clinicians do not prefer to use it (Pekarik, 1985b; Pekarik & Finney-Owen, 1987) and a large percentage have had little or no training in brief therapy (Levonson, Speed, & Budman, 1992).

The great majority of clinicians have been trained and acculturated in the standard therapy model, even though most are now doing some form of brief treatment. There is a great need to retrain current practitioners in brief therapy and integrate brief therapy training into graduate and professional school curricula. Unfortunately, there has been very little research that has addressed brief therapy training methods. Those studies that have done so have demonstrated that such training can improve therapist attitudes toward brief therapy (Levenson & Bolter, 1988) and, more importantly, treatment impact. Both Burlingame et al. (1989) and Pekarik (1994) report that brief therapy training reduced treatment attrition and improved some aspects of outcome. Pekarik's training also resulted in a substantial increase in the reported clinician use of brief therapy and in client satisfaction with treatment.

Alternative training procedures need to be compared. The Pekarik and Burlingame et al., studies cited above have already identified an important training issue that warrants further investigation: the relative importance of the rationale for brief therapy vs. treatment technique. Burlingame et al. suggest that acceptance of brief therapy's rationale was important to the subsequent effectiveness of brief therapy, while I devoted almost one half of my (Pekarik, 1994) training to rationale issues.

Another potentially important training issue is the impact of supervision and consultation for brief therapy cases. I included small group supervision of brief therapy cases subsequent to the didactic workshop-style training in my 1994 study. Trainees' testimonials and my own impressions strongly suggest that this was an important aspect of the training, though this was not systematically assessed. Based on my experience, I currently recommend some form of small group supervision and/or peer consultation regarding uses of brief therapy. Trainees enthusiastically participated in these meetings, both asking for help with difficult cases and sharing their new skill developments with others. Meeting as infrequently as an hour and a half per month seemed to be helpful, so major time commitment to this type of activity may not be needed.

Although very little research has been published on brief therapy training, there are some consistencies across reports. All three of the studies cited earlier found training to be effective in a variety of ways. So there is reason to believe that at least some forms of brief therapy training are beneficial to therapists and their clients. Also encouraging is the fact that the Burlingame et al. (1989) and Pekarik (1994) training achieved their effects with ten to 12 hour programs.

A larger literature on clinical training exists which suggests that certain particular procedures should be employed in any training. Albert and Edelstein (1990) recommend the use of instruction, modeling, feedback, and practice. Each was included in the Pekarik (1994) brief therapy training discussed in this section. Because of the good results achieved by this training and its similarity to the contents of this book, I will present an elaborate description of that training content and format. It is presented as one possible model for training and a source for stimulating thought about alternative training procedures. The training format and outcome will be described first, followed by content description.

Pekarik's (1994) Brief Therapy Training Research

In this study, 22 therapists and 190 of their adult clients participated at three public mental health clinics. The therapists, who had a wide range of experience and approaches to therapy, were randomly assigned to a brief therapy training (n=12 therapists) or control (n=10) condition. Three months after training, clients of trained and control therapists were recruited into an outcome study and served, along with therapists, as the participants in this research (clients were not recruited until three months after training in order to guard against transient training effects). Clients and therapists completed outcome measures at intake, ten weeks after intake, and five months after intake; clients completed satisfaction ratings at ten-week and five-month post-intake. The Brief Symptom Inventory (Derogatis & Spencer, 1982), Mintz & Kiesler's (1982) Target Complaints, and the Client Satisfaction Questionnaire (Attkisson & Zwick, 1982) were the main dependent measures. Before data was analyzed, it was found that there were no intake-level differences between the clients of trained and control therapists, and that the client-participants were representative of outpatients at participating clinics. Also, there were no prestudy differences between the two therapist groups on demographic, treatment duration, or dropout measures.

Trained clinicians reported a doubling of their use of brief therapy relative to control therapists (with two-thirds vs. one-third of clients). Treatment duration was also more appropriate for the trained clinicians: average number of sessions for brief and standard therapy was 4.9 and 11.3 sessions, respectively, for trainees' clients and 5.4 and 7.6 sessions for controls' clients. This suggests that trainees had a better conceptualization of the type of treatment they delivered. Training also apparently made therapists more optimistic about treatment for their clients: although intake scores on all measures were the same for trainees' and controls' clients, trainees gave their clients a better prognosis at intake.

Client satisfaction was most clearly and pervasively affected by the training. Trainees' clients reported greater satisfaction on all four questions of the satisfaction survey at either ten-week or five-month follow-up. They also reported lower dropout rates and a lower proportion cited treatment dissatisfaction as a termination reason. In sum, every one of the satisfaction-relevant measures used in the study was superior for the trainees' clients. One of the three outcome measures (Therapist Ratings) was superior for trainees' clients as well.

The results suggest that training had some very meaningful effects on both therapists and their clients. Therapists used brief therapy more often and, apparently, more appropriately. The length of treatment data for the groups indicates that the trainees had a better conceptualization of the distinction between brief and standard therapy. The effects of training on client satisfaction were most impressive. Clients were "blind" to their therapists' training and control status, yet were pervasively impacted by it. These results were all the more impressive given the extent of the training: a seven-hour workshop followed by two one- and a half-hour group supervision meetings, one held 30 days after training and the other 60 days after training. An outline of the group supervision meetings is presented in Appendix B.

The content of the workshop was essentially the content of this book. It emphasized the rationale presented in Chapter Two, followed by the common abbreviating strategies of (a) rapid assessment and case conceptualization; (b) identification of a narrow focus; (c) negotiation of treatment goals and duration; and (d) a description of how to adapt traditional techniques to a brief format. This, then, supplied initial instruction. As in this book, a case was presented to trainees, who were asked to apply the abbreviation strategies to the client's problems. Modeling, practice, and some feedback were supplied by this aspect of training. Further practice and feedback were provided by the two group supervisory sessions.

The findings of the related research project suggest that the single most likely effect of the procedures in this book is an increase in client satisfaction. This is entirely understandable given the emphasis placed on client preferences. It would not be predicted by those who equate brief treatment with managed care or inferior treatment, however.

There are many different approaches to doing brief therapy that are available in text, video, and workshop formats. As noted earlier, there are approaches that derive from almost every theoretical orientation, so every practitioner should be able to find brief therapy training that speaks his or her theoretical language. But there is a disadvantage to this also: virtually every approach to brief therapy training is affiliated with some particular theoretical orientation, and will not speak the theoretical language of all practitioners. This orientation incompatibility is reduced, but not eliminated, by some of the more eclectic brief therapy approaches. Treatment techniques must come from somewhere, and the traditional therapy approaches are the source. While it is possible to describe treatment technique in generic terms for theoretical purposes (as done in Chapter Eight), this would be quite difficult and unwieldy for detailed description of clinical applications. It would also have the drawback of lacking empirical support, since all the well-executed outcome research has been done with therapies affiliated with traditional orientations. This orientation-affiliation is an advantage to the individual clinician who seeks training as long as the prospective trainee ascertains the theoretical orientation/treatment approach of the trainer or author; it is a disadvantage, however, when a group of clinicians with varying theoretical orientations need to be trained together. As was pointed out in the Preface, this is the case in graduate/professional schools and when training is provided for an entire mental health center or other organized practice site. Given the disinclination of clinicians to buy into novel treatments and theories (Backer, Liberman, & Kuehnel, 1986), the theory-matching problems described above can be a serious obstacle to brief therapy training in some training contexts. A logical strategy is to secure training that is either eclectic or transtheoretical, such as the approach described in this text. Unlike eclecticism, which gathers technique from two or more approaches, a transtheoretical approach builds a theory about how psychotherapies operate in general, acknowledging that this is somewhat independent of the validity of the underpinning theories of psychopathology and behavior change associated with each treatment approach. As illustrated throughout this book, I believe there are distinct advantages to focusing on a general theory and associated techniques of treatment abbreviation.

Appendix A

Case Two

Like the other case examples I have used, this does not depict a real client, but was created for this book. It does, however, accurately depict the nature of cases and their brief therapy. This client had called the clinic one week prior to her first session, requesting treatment for depression. That and demographic information were all that the therapist knew about her before the first session. The following information was provided in the first 40 minutes of a scheduled 50- minute session.

Mary is a 52-year-old administrative assistant who has an 18-year-old daughter and has been married for 20 years. She attended her first session in the middle of a scheduled four-week workplace shutdown and employee work break. Her presenting problem was depression. Symptoms at the first session included frequent crying, low energy, very sad affect, and a reported lack of pleasure and participation in previously enjoyed activities. She met DSM-IV criteria for major depressive disorder. She reported having been depressed to varying degrees much of the time since she had coronary bypass surgery four years earlier. Mary reported she had had acceptable adjustment previous to that with no previous episodes of depression.

Her current depression worsens when she has symptoms reminiscent of those that led to her heart problem diagnosis (e.g., shortness of breath, rapid heartbeat). Her current very sad affect began about four weeks prior to seeking treatment, immediately after a routine examination by her cardiologist. At that visit, she asked if he was going to use an angiogram or rely on the routine, less invasive, exam. She reports that he replied that he would rely on the routine exam, adding "besides, there's no telling what I might find in there." She interpreted this as an indication that her heart was in very bad condition. It "confirmed" what she had frequently ruminated since her surgery: that she was doomed to have another, and deadly, heart attack in the near future. She was so stunned by the physician's words that she had not asked for clarification. Since then, she has been preoccupied with thoughts of death, sadness over what she believes will be a very short life, and worry about how her family will cope after she dies.

Mary's insurance paid for 100 percent of the first three sessions and 50 percent of sessions four to fifteen. Because of Mary's accumulated debt, the 50 percent co-payment would be a major financial burden. Even though she was very depressed, she requested that therapy be limited to eight to ten sessions.

SESSION ONE–CONCEPTUALIZATION

This case presented an interesting set of challenges for any therapy, but especially for brief therapy. Given the severity of depression and the complication of physical problems, it was not at all certain that treatment should be brief. The therapist had to be prepared to consider a negotiated lower treatment fee or some other means of continuing treatment if needed beyond the eighth session.

Conceptualizing Mary's problems and identifying a focus was quite complicated. Potential foci included Mary's:

- imminent death
- shortened life span
- existential grappling with death
- physical limitations due to her heart problems
- state of depression

Review of the focus priorities presented in Chapter Six and the general intervention model presented in Chapter Eight suggests the possibility of a two-stage approach to treating Mary: first focus on the current crisis that involves her concerns about death, then address the depression. More information is needed about both these potential foci before proceeding, however.

[The reader is invited to consider how you would handle this case if it were yours. What information would you seek from Mary? What intervention might you consider for today, in the first session, given that you are in the 40th minute of a scheduled 50 minute session?]

The therapist was fairly sure that Mary either heard her physician incorrectly or that he was attempting to be humorous with his remark about what he might find during an examination. Because clarification of the physician's remarks could possibly have an important impact on Mary's mood, the therapist decided that everything possible should be done to obtain such a clarification as soon as possible. This single step had such potential for alleviating this client's severe suffering that the therapist decided to address this issue before the end of the session. The physician's comment became the *focus* of the latter part of the session, and the *goal* was to clarify it or create a strategy for clarifying it by the end of the first session. This was a *crisis intervention with a clear-cut focus and goal*; as is often the case with crisis intervention, it was hoped that the intervention would restore the client to a precrisis level of adjustment (that level was superior to current adjustment but still depressed, so further treatment would also be needed). The therapist wished to have adequate time for addressing the focus and goal, so he did something unusual 45 minutes into the session—he called the receptionist and told her to inform his next scheduled client that the therapist would be half an hour late for his appointment, i.e., the therapist allotted an extra 45 minutes for Mary.

Although eager to clarify the cardiologist's comments, the therapist was cautious about the impact of a clarification. Even if the cardiologist were to state that Mary misinterpreted him and she was in relatively good physical condition, the client still faced an existential crisis—she had increased her awareness of her mortality and of a shortened life. Even if death were not imminent, Mary was at risk for a shortened life. What remained at issue was *how much* her life was probably shortened. Recall also that even before the cardiologist's recent comments, Mary had concerns about premature death. Mary was in a very depressed state, so even very good news might not have a positive impact. Finally, though unlikely, it was possible that the cardiologist actually did think that Mary's physical condition was poor. In summary, while it was important to clarify the comments, the therapist had to guard against expecting too much from the clarification.

Interventions

High levels of empathy and concern were expressed throughout the first session: special attention was given to the provision of such procedures as eye contact, trunk lean, use of a low even-voiced tone, a furrowed brow, the paraphrase, and reflection of emotion. Emphasis was on the meaning of life and death from Mary's perspective and the implications for how Mary would lead the rest of her life. Comparisons were gently made between her plight and the ultimate plight of everyone, i.e., the certainty of death. These procedures addressed several common therapeutic elements discussed in Chapter Eight and are consistent with recommendations for treating loss and death provided by other authors (e.g., Kübler-Ross, 1975).

After this discussion and associated affective expression, the therapist and Mary drew up a series of questions to ask her physician in order to clarify the assessment of her health, including the relationship of symptoms such as her breathing and heart rate to health. These were written down by the therapist, who advised Mary to pose the questions to her doctor and make *sure* that each one was answered clearly to her satisfaction. The questions were role-played in the session to ensure Mary could do this. The therapist asked Mary if she wanted to make the clarification phone call during the session—then and there. Mary had an appointment with this doctor two days after this session however, and wanted to ask the clarification questions then. The therapist emphasized the importance of posing these questions. Mary's right to know her condition was emphasized, not an expectation that her condition was better than suspected. The therapist asked Mary to call him if she wished after the visit with the physician. More generally, he communicated that he would be very accessible during this crisis.

SESSION TWO

At Session Two Mary reported that she had misunderstood her physician's remarks: at her visit with him, he stated that there were no current indications of cardiovascular problems and her recovery has been a good one so far. She was relieved by this, but still very depressed and tearful. Her current (revised) understanding of her state of health and (less likely) death imminence were discussed. She reported continued fear that the heart problems might reappear; these fearful thoughts were often precipitated by heavy breathing during physical exertion and when she noticed her heartbeat. She had asked her physician (during the "clarification visit") if the presence of accelerated heart rate and breathing during exertion were actual indicators of heart problems, and was told they were not. So a brief cognitive intervention was done: the therapist noted that Mary has been hypersensitive to her heartbeat and breathing and has automatically told herself that these were indicators of ill health. Mary was asked to use these experiences as a cue to tell herself that these are normal and that they are not predictive of worsened health.

There were good reasons for Mary to worry about premature death: she had suffered a serious cardiovascular dysfunction and both of her parents had died of cardiovascular disorders in their early sixties. She was clearly shaken by the vision of her death and very upset over it. Even though she conceded that the probability of imminent death was considerably less than she imagined earlier, she (rationally) concluded that her life might end prematurely. When asked what concerned her most about that prospect, she said that she worried about her family's ability to cope without her. After she identified some specific ways that her husband and daughter might struggle, the therapist asked if she would be reassured if her family said that they could learn to cope in those areas without her; she said that this would indeed make her feel better. Although Mary claimed that her husband was negative toward psychotherapy in general, she thought he might attend a session if it would help her. So Mary was asked to invite her husband to the next session with the goal of addressing her concerns about the family (her daughter was out of town visiting relatives at this time).

Most of the rest of the session was spent with Mary discussing essentially, the life she had led, her regrets, satisfactions, and so on. Mary had not done this since her heart problems became known, nor had she discussed her fears in depth for her family.

During this session, Mary asserted that she did not wish to use psychoactive medications because of the other medication she was already taking for her medical problems.

SESSION THREE

Mary's husband, Frank, accompanied Mary to the session but was only available for one-half hour because of work constraints. He was very concerned about Mary, said he wanted to do what he could to help, but stated he did not want to get involved in a course of counseling. Mary and Frank disclosed that a few days previous they had discussed Mary's concerns about her family's ability to cope if she were to die. Mary had identified several areas of particular concern (e.g., finances) and the two of them discussed what steps could be taken to cope with them. The couple reviewed the most important of these during the session, with Frank taking the lead in reassuringly stating what could be done to cope. They created a plan to have a family discussion about these matters when their daughter returned home the following week. A rationale for presenting this discussion to the daughter and some ways to proceed with the meeting were also discussed.

Mary was occasionally tearful during this part of the session, but said she was reassured by the discussion and was relieved to have a plan for a similar discussion with her daughter. Mary seemed to have gained some closure on the existential and practical issues regarding her medical condition by the latter part of this session. She expressed an accurate view of her situation, which was that her life expectancy was shorter than it would have been without her ailments, but that dying was not an imminent prospect—many more years of living were probable.

Though not distraught over dying, Mary was still quite depressed and wondered why. This was an appropriate place for the therapist and Mary to move from dealing with the emergent crisis (based on fear of death and unresolved existential issues) to the treatment of the longer-standing depression. The therapist provided a cognitive-behavioral-biological explanation of depression tailored to her situation, then asked her about engagement in social, recreational, and pleasurable activities. She reported she engaged in virtually no pleasurable activity, though she had a wide range of interests and recreation she had enjoyed before her depression.

The therapist emphasized the reciprocal relationship between depression and activity. He asked Mary to record (1) pleasurable acts in the next week and (2) both the best and worst mood each day, using a 1 to 10 mood scale (10 = best). He also asked if her concerns continued to mount when she experienced increased heart and breathing rates. She said she had been getting better at reducing this problem by using the cognitive intervention from the previous week. Lastly, the therapist asked Mary to identify some easily accomplished pleasant activities (e.g., call a friend, eat a favorite food) and engage in one or two of them in the next seven days.

SESSION FOUR

This was the first session during which Mary was not tearful or crying. She reported being less depressed than she had been since the problematic cardiologist visit, though still depressed. She had engaged in pleasurable activities twice in the past week—a phone call to a friend and shopping for clothes—and found them mildly enjoyable. Much of the session was devoted to further discussion of interests and potentially enjoyable activities. A calendar of activities was devised with one particular activity identified for each day of the week. A list of alternative activities was generated in case Mary was not in the mood for a scheduled activity or if it proved not feasible. Because Mary's recent existence had been so anhedonic, the therapist encouraged Mary to recall details of past pleasures and fantasize about future ones during the session.

Her daily mood record indicated that she had very low moods daily; she added that she usually cried at these times. She noted that a "3" was her threshold for feeling tearful or crying. Encouragingly, she said that the lowest moods typically lasted less than an hour. Her record also noted the occurrence of relatively good moods on four of seven days—indicated by a "6" or higher—and she was encouraged by this.

Self-statements had continued to be effective at stopping physiological arousal from eliciting thoughts that her heart problems were returning. Mary revealed that her low moods were accompanied and sometimes precipitated by depressive thoughts (primarily related to concerns about family, shortened life, and quality of life). Most of these had been previously addressed in therapy but they intruded "automatically." She and the therapist further discussed logical and depression-inhibiting alternative ways of considering these issues; the therapist recommended she use her low moods as a cue to identify depression-engendering thoughts and replace them with the alternatives discussed in session. Mary was very good at identifying, disputing, and replacing irrational thoughts during the session, leading her therapist to believe that cognitions (other than those addressing a cardiac relapse, which were being handled adequately) were somewhat less important than Mary's lack of pleasant activity.

Mary reported that she, her husband, and daughter had a family discussion about how they would cope if Mary were to die or be disabled. The family was supportive and convinced Mary that they could cope in her absence; Mary seemed very reassured by the family meeting. Activities with her daughter were scheduled for two days in the coming week as part of "pleasant activities." Mary agreed to bring her daughter to a session at some point.

SESSION FIVE

In Session Five, Mary reported significant improvement that was supported by her daily mood report: only three of seven days had a "3" or lower, and six of seven days had a "6" or higher during some portion of the day. She enjoyed her assigned activities and engaged in six of the seven assigned. The session was primarily devoted to "brainstorming" other, more energy-demanding pleasant activities, and fitting them into a daily schedule. Favored activities included those she could do on her own (such as shopping), but emphasized social activities such as going to lunch, making phone calls, and visiting friends and family. A written schedule was again created and Mary was asked to return it next session with an indication of actual activity. She was encouraged to substitute or add new pleasant activities during the week. She reported only transient depressive moods in the previous week. Mary continued to be adept at catching her illogical depressive thoughts and disputing them. Because Mary seemed emotionally stronger, the therapist asked about the prospects of including her husband in her pleasant activities. Mary said that they had few common interests and that both before and after her medical problems they shared few recreational activities. She had neither the desire nor emotional stability to tackle this issue.

SESSION SIX

In Session Six, Mary complained of a major disappointment: she revealed that her enjoyment of sexual activity had not returned as hoped. Her family doctor had been consulted (unbeknownst to the therapist) and he recommended that she watch "sexy videos" to heighten her sexual interest. When this failed, she confessed to her husband that her sexual interest was low; this distressed him and made her even more upset. She had been prescribed sex hormones about one year previous, but ceased taking them due to side effects. They had had a beneficial effect on her sexual appetite when she took them.

The relationship between sexual enjoyment, general activity level, and depression was described by the therapist. It was suggested that a continued increase in enjoyable activities and a decrease in depression might lead to an increase in libido. Furthermore, it was suggested that the next week or two might be a good time to use a lower dose of the sex hormone: the lower dose would avoid side effects but still might be strong enough to increase libido due to the recent salutary effect of lowered depression and increased activity. Mary was advised to call her physician and request an appropriate prescription.

SESSION SEVEN

In Session Seven, Mary reported that a different sex hormone, less likely to cause side effects was prescribed and use was begun two days previous. While no immediate effects were apparent, the client was generally hopeful of return of libido due to continued lessening of depression and increase in activity. Mary engaged in all the prescribed activities, plus she added some on her own; she reported enjoying these activities very much. More enjoyable activities were identified.

By this time, she had a large repertoire and was very good at devising scheduled activities on her own. Her affect appeared normal and she reported very few depressive feelings during the previous week.

SESSION EIGHT

Session Eight occurred two weeks after Session Seven due to scheduling difficulties. Mary reported no clinically significant depression and noted a significant increase in sexual enjoyment. She continued enjoyment of scheduled activities and was now devising the schedule all on her own.

She reported some concern over a work-related problem with her supervisor. Possible ways of coping with it were discussed.

Mary appeared to be able to cope well with situations and was no longer clinically depressed, although she occasionally had brief sad moods caused by thought of the return of heart ailments and a shortened life.

Mary introduced a new concern: her daughter had decided not to enroll at college as planned and Mary feared this was due to concerns about Mary's heart problems and depression. Mary was interested in inviting her daughter to a session to address this issue, so this was planned for the following meeting, which was scheduled for two weeks later to evaluate Mary's capacity for coping with problems on her own.

SESSION NINE

At Session Nine, adjustment continued to be good. Mary's daughter, Sarah, attended and appeared to have a good relationship with Mary. She seemed to genuinely want to take a year off from school for sound personal reasons (not ready for school, wanted to save money, had a job she liked, worked with friends). Sarah's presence allowed a review of her feelings about Mary and her illness. Both Mary and Sarah were expressive and positive about their relationship during the discussion. Although Mary preferred that Sarah go off to college, she accepted the decision to delay college.

Sarah left the session with about 15 minutes remaining. During that time, the course of treatment was reviewed and effective components were identified. Mary expressed a desire to continue scheduling activities, but felt competent to do so on her own (as she had demonstrated for weeks). Because of the numerous issues in Mary's life, a final half-hour session was scheduled two weeks following.

SESSION TEN

Mary reported that her adjustment remained good since her last session. She described irritation with her job supervisor, but acknowledged this was a normal problem of living and not particularly bothersome. Significant improvement had been reported and observed since the fifth session, 11 weeks previous. Both Mary and her therapist regarded her adjustment as relatively stable, so it was agreed to terminate treatment. Things Mary could do to maintain her good adjustment were identified, as were indicators of depression that would signal a need to return to treatment. The therapist's accessibility for dealing with future upsets was strongly emphasized.

Note: Although not reflected in the above session-by-session account, a number of fairly minor problems were raised and addressed throughout treatment. For example, practical obstacles to participation in the enjoyable activities and distorted body image due to some weight gain and surgical scars were referred to frequently. These issues were dealt with in a compassionate but rational and problem-solving manner. This attitude, together with accessibility and flexibility in dealing with issues clearly relevant to the treatment focus, are regarded as important ingredients in the success of this case. On the other hand, the therapist avoided digression into areas not clearly focus-related. For example, in the middle sessions it was clear that Mary's husband was somewhat inflexible in adapting his schedule to Mary's increased desire for recreational activity. Because Mary reported that this had been the case for most of their 20-year marriage, Mary and the therapist "worked around" this obstacle—she increased her recreational activities with people other than her husband. As another (related) example, Mary's husband was shocked when she informed him of her lack of sexual enjoyment (Session Five). Apparently, communication regarding sexual matters was inadequate. Since this, too, was a long-standing phenomenon and not a critical contributor to her depression, it was not addressed extensively.

Appendix B

Guidelines for Group Supervision of Brief Therapy Cases

Purpose of follow-up training:

(1) To supplement workshop or text training in brief therapy.
(2) To give therapists supervised practice in use of brief therapy procedures.
(3) To keep ongoing awareness of brief therapy principles and provide incentive to use them.

Nature of follow-up training: Case presentation/group supervision; three to ten therapists per group. One to two hours is a suitable duration for each meeting.

Timing: The first training session, usually a group supervision, should occur some time after initial text or workshop training. The ideal time is after therapists have had a chance to pick up at least two new cases on which to consider the use of brief therapy. Usually this is about two to three weeks after initial training.

Second follow-up should be two to three weeks after the first. Subsequent follow-up meetings should occur at three to four week intervals.

Content: In the past, I have asked each therapist in attendance to very briefly describe the new cases to which the brief therapy strategy has or might be applied. After all therapists have done this, one or two longer presentations are requested from attendees. Therapists should be told beforehand to come prepared to discuss application of brief therapy to their new cases and bring relevant case material.

Priority topics for presentation:

(1) Cases to which the brief therapy strategy has been successfully applied.
(2) Cases that appear to be appropriate for brief therapy, but the therapist has some difficulty in application (problems identifying an appropriately narrow focus are especially common).
(3) Cases in which the therapist is unsure regarding the appropriateness of brief therapy.
(4) Cases that could be approached using either brief therapy or standard therapy.
(5) Cases for which the therapist has difficulty deciding between two or more brief treatment strategies.

Topics 2 through 5 will be most common and appropriate during the first follow-up session or two. Trainers should encourage a brain-storming, problem-solving approach wherein all therapists in the group act as "therapists" for the identified case and propose the treatment plan and strategy they would use.

Trainers should be flexible and encourage several possible approaches to the same case, avoiding the idea that there is only one right way to approach the case.

The experience of a planned one- to two-session treatment course will probably be reported by some therapists in the first follow-up meeting or two. This should be encouraged by asking the therapists involved to share their conceptualization and treatment procedures with the group. The trainer can keep a list of such cases and thereby create a (growing) group of such cases. Gradually, a list of the types of cases (problems and client characteristics) appropriate for a planned one to two visit treatment course can be generated to guide therapists in the selection of cases for very brief therapy.

Trainers should try to avoid the all-too-frequent case conference atmosphere of a single therapist simply exhibiting his or her accomplishments. While (praise and) recognition of the use of brief therapy tactics is especially important in early training sessions, more learning and interest will be accomplished by the group's participation in the vicarious treatment of cases.

In later training sessions, successful brief therapy applications can be described. The problem-solving group participation can be encouraged in later sessions by inclusion of case presentations in which the therapist (a) is unsure how to proceed in the later stages of treatment, (b) has difficulty terminating, or (c) wishes to retrospectively consider an alternative treatment strategy.

After two or three sessions, it is likely that the therapists will start to use the group as a place to develop a range of related clinic and treatment improvements. Suggestions for short-term groups, changes in intake procedures and paperwork, training needs, research needs, ways of rewarding effective brief treatment, and other such issues may be raised and can improve clinic functioning.

References

American Psychological Association (1992). Ethical principles of psychologists and code of conduct. *American Psychologist, 47,* 1597-1611.

Acosta, F. X. (1980). Self-described reasons for premature termination of psychotherapy by Mexican American, Black American, and Anglo-American patients. *Psychological Reports, 47,* 435-443.

Albert, G., & Edelstein, B. (1990). Therapist training: A critical review of skill training studies. *Clinical Psychology Review, 10,* 497-511.

Arnkoff, D. B., Victor, B., & Glass, C. (1993). Empirical research on factors in psychotherapeutic change. In *Comprehensive handbook of psychotherapy integration,* G. Stricker & J. R. Gold (Eds.), (pp. 27-42). New York: Plenum.

Attkisson, C. C., & Zwick, R. (1982). The client satisfaction questionnaire: Psychometric properties and correlations with service utilization and psychotherapy outcome. *Evaluation and Program Planning, 5,* 223-237.

Backer, T. E., Liberman, R. P., & Kuehnel, T. G. (1986). Dissemination and adoption of innovative psychosocial interventions. *Journal of Consulting and Clinical Psychology, 54,* 111-118.

Baekeland, F., & Lundwall, L. (1975). Dropping out of treatment: A critical review. *Psychological Bulletin, 82,* 738-783.

Baldwin, B. A. (1977). Crisis intervention in professional practice: Implications for clinical training. *American Journal of Orthopsychiatry, 47,* 659-670.

Baldwin, B. A. (1979). Crisis intervention: An overview of theory and practice. *The Counseling Psychologist, 8,* 43-52.

Balint, M., Ornstein, P. H., & Balint, E. (1972). *Focal psychotherapy: An example of applied psychoanalysis.* London: Lippincott.

Bateson, G. (1979). *Steps to an ecology of mind.* New York: Ballantine.

Beck, A. T., Rush, A. J., Shaw, B. R., & Emery, G. (1979). *Cognitive therapy of depression: A treatment manual.* New York: Guilford Press.

Bellak, L. (1984). Intensive brief and emergency psychotherapy. In *Psychiatry update: The American Psychiatric Association Annual Review* Vol. III, L. Grinspoon (Ed.), (pp. 11-24). Washington, DC: American Psychiatric Press.

Bellak, L., & Small, L. (1965). *Emergency psychotherapy and brief psychotherapy.* New York: Grune & Stratton.

Bellak, L., & Small, L. (1978). *Emergency psychotherapy and brief psychotherapy* (2nd ed.). New York: Grune & Stratton.

Benbenishty, R., & Schul, Y. (1987). Client-therapist congruence of expectations over the course of therapy. *British Journal of Clinical Psychology, 26,* 17-24.

Benson, H. (1975). *The relaxation response.* New York: Morrow.

Bergin, A. E., & Garfield, S. L. (1994). Overview, trends, & future issues. In *Handbook of psychotherapy and behavior change*, A. E. Bergin, & S. L. Garfield (Eds.), 4th ed., pp. 821-830). New York: Wiley.

Beutler, L. E., Machado, P. P., & Neufeldt, S. (1994). Therapist variables. In *Handbook of psychotherapy and behavior change*, A. E. Bergin, & S. L. Garfield (Eds.), (4th ed., pp. 229-269). New York: Wiley.

Blackwell, B. (1976). Treatment adherence. *British Journal of Psychiatry, 129*, 513-531.

Blake, D. D., Abueg, F. R., Woodward, S. H., & Keane, T. M. (1993). Treatment efficacy in posttraumatic stress disorder. In *Handbook of effective psychotherapy*, T. R. Giles (Ed.), (pp. 195-226). New York: Plenum.

Bloom, B. L. (1979). *Community mental health: A general introduction*. Monterey, CA: Brooks/Cole.

Bloom, B. L. (1981). Focused single-session therapy: Initial development and evaluation. In *Forms of brief therapy*, S. Budman (Ed.), (pp. 167-216). New York: Guilford Press.

Bloom, B. L. (1984). *Community mental health: A general introduction* (2nd ed.). Monterey, CA: Brooks/Cole.

Bloom, B. L. (1992). *Planned short-term psychotherapy: A clinical handbook*. Boston: Allyn & Bacon.

Bolter, K., Levenson, H., & Alvarez, W. (1990). Differences in values between short-term and long-term therapists. *Professional Psychology: Research and Practice, 21*, 285-290.

Budman, S. H., & Gurman, A. S. (1983). The practice of brief psychotherapy. *Professional Psychology: Research and Practice, 14*, 177-182.

Budman, S. H., & Gurman, A. S. (1988). *Theory and practice of brief therapy*. New York: Guilford Press.

Budman, S. H., Hoyt, M. F., & Friedman, S. (Eds.). (1992). *The first session in brief therapy*. New York: Guilford.

Burlingame, G., Fuhriman, A., Paul, S., & Ogles, B. M. (1989). Implementing a time-limited therapy program: Differential effects of training and experience. *Psychotherapy, 26*, 303-313.

Caplan, G. (1963). Types of mental health consultation. *American Journal of Orthopsychiatry, 33*, 470-481.

Caplan, G. (1964). *Principles of preventive psychiatry*. New York: Basic Books.

Carmona, P. E. (1988). Changing traditions in psychotherapy: A study of therapists' attitudes. *Clinical Nurse Specialist, 2*, 185-190.

Chambless, D. (chair). (1993). Task force on promotion and dissemination of psychological procedures. Division 12, American Psychological Association.

Corsini, R. J. (1991). *Five therapists and one client*. Itasca, IL: Peacock Publishers.

Cummings, N. A. (1977a). The anatomy of psychotherapy under national health insurance. *American Psychologist, 32*, 711-718.

Cummings, N. A. (1977b). Prolonged (ideal) versus short-term (realistic) psychotherapy. *Professional Psychology, 8*, 491-501.

Cummings, N. A. (1995). Behavioral health after managed care: The next golden opportunity for professional psychology. *The Register Report, 20 & 21*, 1, 30-33.

Cummings, N. A., & Follette, W. T. (1968). Psychiatric services and medical utilization in a prepaid health plan setting: Part II. *Medical Care, 6*, 31-41.

Davanloo, H. (Ed.). (1978). *Basic principles and techniques in short-term dynamic psychotherapy.* New York: Spectrum.

Derogatis, L., & Spencer, P. (1982). *The brief symptom inventory: Administration, scoring and procedures manual-I*, Baltimore, MD: Clinical Psychometric Research.

De Shazer, S. (1985). *Keys to solution in brief therapy.* New York: Norton.

Duehn, W. D., & Proctor, E. K. (1977). Initial client interaction and premature discontinuance in treatment. *American Journal of Orthopsychiatry, 47*, 284-290.

Dunbar, J. M., & Agras, W. S. (1980). Compliance with medical instructions. In *The comprehensive handbook of behavioral medicine*, J. M. Ferguson, & C. B. Taylor (Eds.), (pp. 115-145). New York: Spectrum.

D'Zurilla, T. J., & Goldfried, M. R. (1971). Problem-solving and behavior modification. *Journal of Abnormal Psychology, 78*, 107-126.

Edwards, G., Orford, J., Egert, S., Guthrie, S., Hawker, A., Hensman, D., Mitcheson, M., Oppenheimer, E., & Taylor, C. (1977). Alcoholism: A controlled trial of "treatment" and "advice." *Journal of Studies on Alcohol, 38*, 1004-1031.

Egan, G. (1982). *The skilled helper* (2nd ed.). Monterey, CA: Brooks/Cole.

Ellis, A., & Harper, R. A. (1975). *A new guide to rational living.* North Hollywood, CA: Wilshire.

Epperson, D. L., Bushway, D. J., & Warman, R. E. (1983). Client self-terminations after one counseling session: Effects of problem recognition, counselor gender, and counselor experience. *Journal of Counseling Psychology, 30*, 307-315.

Epstein, N. B., Bishop, D. S., Keitner, G. I., & Miller, I. (1990). A systems therapy: Problem-centered systems therapy of the family. In *Handbook of brief psychotherapies*, R. A. Wells, & V. J. Giannetti (Eds.), (pp. 405-436). New York: Plenum.

Erickson, M. H. (1967). *Advanced techniques of hypnosis and therapy: Selected papers of M. H. Erickson.* J. Haley, Ed. New York: Grune & Stratton.

Erikson, E. H. (1959). Identity and the life cycle. *Psychological Issues.* Monograph 1, 1 (1). New York: International Universities Press.

Follette, W., & Cummings, N. A. (1967). Psychiatric services and medical utilization in a prepaid health plan setting. *Medical Care, 5*, 25-35.

Frank, J. D. (1982). Therapeutic components shared by all psychotherapies. In *The master lecture series (Vol. 1) Psychotherapy research and behavior change.* J. H. Harvey & M. M. Parks (Eds.), (pp. 9-37). Washington, DC: American Psychological Association.

Frank, R. G., & Vandenbos, G. R. (1994). Health care reform: The 1993-1994 evolution. *American Psychologist, 49*, 851-854.

Garfield, S. L. (1963). A note on patients' reasons for terminating therapy. *Psychological Reports, 13*, 38.

Garfield, S. L. (1980). *Psychotherapy: An eclectic approach.* New York: Wiley.

Garfield, S. L. (1986). Research on client variables in psychotherapy. In *Handbook of psychotherapy and behavior change*, S. L. Garfield, & A. E. Bergin (Eds.), (3rd ed., pp. 213-256). New York: Wiley.

Garfield, S. L. (1994). Research on client variables in psychotherapy. In *Handbook of psychotherapy and behavior change*, A. E. Bergin, & S. L. Garfield (Eds.), (4th ed., pp. 190-228). New York: Wiley.

Garfield, S. L., & Wolpin, M. (1963). Expectations regarding psychotherapy. *Journal of Nervous and Mental Disease, 137*, 353-362.

Gelfand, D. M., & Hartmann, D. P. (1984). *Child behavior analysis and therapy* (2nd ed.). New York: Pergamon.

Gelso, C. J., & Johnson, D. H. (1983). *Explorations in time-limited counseling and psychotherapy.* New York: Teachers College Press.

Getz, W. L., Fujita, B. N., & Allen, D. (1975). The use of paraprofessionals in crisis intervention: Evaluation of an innovative program. *American Journal of Community Psychology, 3*, 135-144.

Giannetti, V. (1990). Brief treatment and mental health policy. In *Handbook of the brief psychotherapies*, R. A. Wells, & V. J. Giannetti (Eds.), (pp. 79-92). New York: Plenum.

Giles, T. R. (Ed.). (1993). *Handbook of effective psychotherapy.* New York: Plenum.

Goldfried, M. R. (1980). Psychotherapy as coping skills training. In *Psychotherapy process: Current issues and future directions*, M. J. Mahoney (Ed.) (pp. 89-119). New York: Plenum Press.

Gottschalk, L., Mayerson, P., & Gottlieb, A. (1967). Prediction and evaluation of outcome in an emergency brief therapy clinic. *Journal of Nervous and Mental Disease, 144*, 77-96.

Grencavage, L. M., & Norcross, J. C. (1990). What are the commonalities among the therapeutic factors? *Professional Psychology: Research and Practice, 21*, 372-378.

Gurman, A. S., & Kniskern, D. P. (1978). Research on marital and family therapy: Progress, perspective and prospect. In *Handbook of psychotherapy and behavior change*, S. L. Garfield, & A. E. Bergin (Eds.), (2nd ed., pp. 817-902). New York: Wiley.

Haaga, D. A., & Davison, G. C. (1986). Cognitive change methods. In *Helping people change*, J. H. Kanfer, & A. P. Goldstein (Eds.), (3rd ed., pp. 236-282). New York: Pergamon Press.

Haas, L. J., & Cummings, N. A. (1991). Managed outpatient mental health plans: Clinical, ethical, and practical guidelines for participation. *Professional Psychology: Research and Practice, 22*, 45-51.

Haley, J. (1973). *Uncommon therapy: The psychiatric techniques of Milton H. Erickson.* New York: Norton.

Heitler, J. B. (1976). Preparatory techniques in initiating expressive psychotherapy with lower class, unsophisticated patients. *Psychological Bulletin, 83,* 339-352.

Hoffman, D. L., & Remmel, M. L. (1975). Uncovering the precipitant in crisis intervention. *Social Casework, 56,* 259-267.

Horenstein, D., & Houston, B. K. (1976). The expectation-reality discrepancy and premature termination from psychotherapy. *Journal of Clinical Psychology, 32,* 373-378.

Hornstra, R., Lubin, R., Lewis, R., & Willis, B. (1972). Worlds apart: Patients and professionals. *Archives of General Psychiatry, 27,* 553-557.

Houpt, J. L., Orleans, C. S., George, L. K., & Brodie, H. K. (1979). *The importance of mental health services to general health care.* Cambridge, MA: Ballinger.

Howard, K. I., Kopta, S. M., Krause, M. S., & Orlinsky, D. E. (1986). The dose-effect relationship in psychotherapy. *American Psychologist, 41,* 159-164.

Howard, K., Lueger, R., Maling, M., & Martinovich, Z. (1993). A phase model of psychotherapy outcome: Causal mediation of change. *Journal of Consulting and Clinical Psychology, 61,* 678-685.

Hoyt, M. F. (1985). Therapist resistances to short-term dynamic psychotherapy. *Journal of the American Academy of Psychoanalysis, 13,* 93-112.

Johnson, D. H., & Gelso, C. J. (1980). The effectiveness of time limits in counseling and psychotherapy: A critical review. *The Counseling Psychologist, 9,* 70-83.

Jones, D. R., & Vischi, R. R. (1979). Impact of alcohol, drug abuse and mental health treatment on medical care utilization: A review of the research literature. *Medical Care, 17* (suppl. 12), 1-82.

Jonson, A. R., Siegler, M., & Winslade, W. J. (1986). *Clinical ethics* (2nd ed.). New York: Macmillan.

Karasu, T. B. (1987). The psychotherapy of the future. *Psychosomatics, 28,* 380-381, 384.

Keith-Spiegel, P., & Koocher, G. P. (1985). *Ethics in psychology.* New York: Random House.

Kiesler, C. A., & Morton, T. L. (1988). Psychology and public policy in the "Health Care Revolution." *American Psychologist, 43,* 993-1003.

Klerman, G. L., Weissman, M., Rousauville, B., & Chevron, E. (1984). *Interpersonal psychotherapy of depression.* New York: Basic Books.

Knesper, D. J., Pagnucco, D. J., & Wheeler, J. R. (1985). Similarities and differences across mental health services providers and practice settings in the United States. *American Psychologist, 40,* 1352-1369.

Kopta, S. M., Howard, K. I., Lawry, J., & Beutler, L. (1994). Patterns of symptomatic recovery in psychotherapy. *Journal of Consulting and Clinical Psychology, 62,* 1009-1016.

Koss, M. P. (1979). Length of psychotherapy for clients seen in private practice. *Journal of Consulting and Clinical Psychology, 47,* 210-212.

Koss, M. P., & Butcher, J. N. (1986). Research on brief therapy. In *Handbook of psychotherapy and behavior change*, S. L. Garfield, & A. E. Bergin (Eds.), (3rd ed., pp. 627-670). New York: Wiley.

Koss, M. P., & Shiang J. (1994). Research on brief psychotherapy. In *Handbook of psychotherapy and behavior change*, A. E. Bergin, & S. L. Garfield (Eds.), (4th ed., pp. 664-700). New York: Wiley.

Kübler-Ross, E. (1975). *Death: The final stage of growth.* Englewood Cliffs, NJ: Prentice-Hall.

Lambert, M. J., & Bergin, A. E. (1994). The effectiveness of psychotherapy. In *Handbook of psychotherapy and behavior change*, S. L. Garfield & A. E. Bergin (Eds.), (4th ed.), (pp. 143-189). New York: Wiley.

Lambert, M. J., Shapiro, D. A., & Bergin, A. E. (1986). The effectiveness of psychotherapy. In *Handbook of psychotherapy and behavior change*, S. L. Garfield & A. E. Bergin (Eds.), (3rd ed., pp. 157-212). New York: Wiley.

Lazarus, A. A. (1981). *The practice of multimodal therapy.* New York: McGraw-Hill.

Lebow, J. (1982). Consumer satisfaction with mental health treatment. *Psychological Bulletin, 91*, 244-259.

Levenson, H., & Bolter, K. (1988, August). *Short-term psychotherapy values and attitudes: Changes with training.* Paper presented at the annual meeting of the American Psychological Association, Atlanta, GA.

Levenson, H., Speed, J. L., & Budman, S. H. (1992, June). *Therapists' training and skill in brief therapy: A survey of Massachusetts and California psychologists.* Paper presented to the Society for Psychotherapy Research, Berkeley, CA.

Lewin, K. K. (1970). *Brief encounters: Brief psychotherapy.* St. Louis, MO: Green.

Lewinsohn, R. M. (1975). The behavioral study and treatment of depression. In *Progress in behavior modification, Vol. 1*, M. Hersen, R. M. Eisler, & P. M. Miller (Eds.). New York: Academic Press.

Lindemann, E. (1994). Symptomatology and management of acute grief. *American Journal of Psychiatry, 101*, 141-148.

Llewelyn, S. P. (1988). Psychological therapy as viewed by clients and therapists. *British Journal of Clinical Psychology, 27*, 223-237.

Luborsky, L., Singer, B., & Luborsky, L. (1975). Comparative studies of psychotherapies. *Archives of General Psychiatry, 32*, 995-1008.

Malan, D. H. (1973). *A study of brief psychotherapy.* New York: Plenum.

Malan, D. H. (1976). *The frontiers of brief psychotherapy: An example of the convergence of research and clinical practice.* New York: Plenum.

Mann, J. (1973). *Time-limited psychotherapy.* Cambridge, MA: Harvard University Press.

Marmor, J. (1979). Short-term dynamic psychotherapy. *American Journal of Psychiatry, 136*, 149-155.

Martin, D. G. (1983). *Counseling and therapy skills.* Prospect Heights, IL: Waveland.

Maslach, C. (1978). The client role in staff burn-out. *Journal of Social Issues, 34*, 111-124.

Matarazzo, R. G., & Patterson, D. (1986). Research on the teaching and learning of therapeutic skills. In *Handbook of psychotherapy and behavior change*, S. L. Garfield & A. E. Bergin (eds.), (3rd ed., pp. 821-844). New York: Wiley.

McGreevy, M. K. (1987). *A survey of psychotherapy expectations and preferences of university students*. Unpublished Master's thesis, Washburn University, Topeka, KS.

Meichenbaum, D. (1985). *Stress inoculation training*. New York: Pergamon Press.

Miller, W. R., Gribskov, D. J., & Mortell, R. L. (1981). Effectiveness of a self-control manual for problem drinkers with and without therapist contact. *International Journal of the Addictions, 16*, 827-837.

Miller, W. R., & Hester, R. K. (1986). Inpatient alcoholism treatment: Who benefits? *American Psychologist, 41*, 794-805.

Miller, W. R., & Taylor, C. A. (1980). Relative effectiveness of bibliotherapy, individual and group self-control training in the treatment of problem drinkers. *Addictive Behaviors, 5*, 13-24.

Miller, W. R., Taylor, C. A., West, J. C. (1980). Focused versus broad-spectrum therapy for problem drinkers. *Journal of Consulting and Clinical Psychology, 48*, 590-601.

Mintz, J., & Kiesler, D. J. (1982). Individualized measures of psychotherapy outcome. In *Handbook of research methods in clinical psychology*, P. C. Kendall & J. N. Butcher (Eds.), (pp. 491-534). New York: Wiley.

Monahan, J. (1984). The prediction of violent behavior: Toward a second generation of theory and policy. *American Journal of Psychiatry, 141*, 10-15.

Morris, R. J., & Kratochwill, T. R. (1991). *The practice of child therapy*. Boston: Allyn & Bacon.

Mumford, E., Schlesinger, H. J., Glass, G. V., Patrick, C., & Cuerdon, T. (1984). A new look at evidence about reduced cost of medical utilization following mental health treatment. *American Journal of Psychiatry, 141*, 1145-1158.

National Center for Health Statistics. (1988). *The national ambulatory medical care survey* (Series 13, No. 93, DHHS Publication No. PHS 88-1754). Washington, DC: U. S. Government Printing Office.

National Institute of Mental Health. (1979). Report of the work group on health insurance, 1974. In *Reporting program evaluations: Two sample community mental health center annual reports*, C. Windle (Ed.). Rockville, MD: U. S. Department of Health, Education and Welfare.

National Institute of Mental Health. (1981). *Provisional data on federally funded community mental health centers, 1978-79*. Report prepared by the Survey and Reports Branch, Division of Biometry and Epidemiology. Washington, DC: U. S. Government Printing Office.

Newman, R., & Bricklin, P. (1991). Parameters of managed mental health care: Legal, ethical, and professional guidelines. *Professional Psychology: Research & Practice, 22*, 26-35.

Nezu, A. M., & Nezu, C. M. (Eds.). (1989). *Clinical decision making in behavior therapy.* Champaign, IL: Research Press.

Norcross, J. C., & Goldfried, M. R. (1992). *Handbook of psychotherapy integration.* New York: Basic Books.

Norcross, J. C., & Wogan, M. (1983). American psychotherapists of diverse persuasion. Characteristics, theories, practices, and clients. *Professional Psychology: Research and Practice, 14,* 529-539.

O'Hanlon, W. H., & Weiner-Davis, M. (1989). *In search of solutions: A new direction in psychotherapy.* New York: W. W. Norton.

Orlinsky, D. E., Grawe, K., & Parks, B. K. (1994). Process and outcome in psychotherapy-noch einmal. In *Handbook of psychotherapy and behavior change,* A. E. Bergin & S. L. Garfield (Eds.), (4th ed., pp. 270-378). New York: Wiley.

Overall, W. C., & Aronson, H. (1962). Expectations of psychotherapy in lower socioeconomic class patients. *American Journal of Orthopsychiatry, 32,* 271-272.

Pekarik, G. (1983a). Follow-up adjustment of outpatient dropouts. *American Journal of Orthopsychiatry, 53,* 501-511.

Pekarik, G. (1983b). Improvement in clients who have given different reasons for dropping out of treatment. *Journal of Clinical Psychology, 39,* 909-913.

Pekarik, G. (1985a). Coping with dropouts. *Professional Psychology: Research and Practice, 16,* 114-123.

Pekarik, G. (1985b). The effects of employing different termination classification criteria in dropout research. *Psychotherapy, 23,* 532-534.

Pekarik, G. (1986). The use of termination status and treatment duration patterns as an indicator of clinical improvement. *Evaluation and Program Planning, 9,* 25-30.

Pekarik, G. (1988). The relationship of counselor identification of client problem description to continuance in a behavioral weight loss program. *Journal of Counseling Psychology, 35,* 66-70.

Pekarik, G. (1990, January). *Rationale for consumer-oriented treatment strategies.* Invited address at the annual executive director's meeting of the Metropolitan Clinics of Counseling (CIGNA Corp.), Phoenix, AZ.

Pekarik, G. (1991a). Relationship of expected and actual treatment duration for child and adult clients. *Journal of Clinical Child Psychology, 20,* 121-125.

Pekarik, G. (1991b). *Treatment impact at managed mental health care clinic.* Unpublished manuscript. Washburn University, Topeka, KS.

Pekarik, G. (1992a). Post-treatment adjustment of clients who drop out early vs. late in treatment. *Journal of Clinical Child Psychology, 48,* 379-388.

Pekarik, G. (1992b). Relationship of clients' reasons for dropping out of treatment to outcome and satisfaction. *Journal of Clinical Psychology, 48,* 91-98.

Pekarik, G. (1993). Beyond effectiveness: Uses of consumer-oriented criteria in defining treatment success. In *Handbook of effective psychotherapy,* T. Giles (Ed.). New York: Plenum.

Pekarik, G. (1994). Effects of brief therapy training on practicing psychotherapists and their clients. *Community Mental Health Journal, 30,* 135-144.

Pekarik, G. (1995). *Psychotherapy attendance patterns in private practice settings.* Unpublished manuscript. Antioch New Enlgand Graduate School, Keene, NH.

Pekarik, G., & Finney-Owen, K. (1987). Psychotherapists' attitudes and beliefs relevant to client dropout. *Community Mental Health Journal, 23,* 120-130.

Pekarik, G., & Tongier, P. (1993, April). *Variables associated with successful and unsuccessful early termination from psychotherapy.* Presented at the Annual Meeting of the Midwestern Psychological Association, Chicago, IL.

Pekarik, G., & Wierzbicki, M. (1986). The relationship between expected and actual psychotherapy duration. *Psychotherapy, 23,* 532-534.

Piper, W. E., Debbane, E. G., Bienvenu, J. P., & Garant, J. (1984). A comparative study of four forms of psychotherapy. *Journal of Consulting and Clinical Psychology, 52,* 268-279.

Prochaska, J. O. (1984). *Systems of psychotherapy* (2nd ed.). Homewood, IL: The Dorsey Press.

Prochaska, J. O., & DiClemente, C. C. (1984). *The transtheoretical approach: Crossing the traditional boundaries of therapy.* Homewood, IL: Dow Jones-Irvin.

Riessman, D. K., Rabkin, J. G., & Struening, E. L. (1977). Brief versus standard psychiatric hospitalization: A critical review of the literature. *Community Mental Health Review, 2,* 2-10.

Rogers, C. R. (1951). *Client-centered therapy.* Boston: Houghton Mifflin.

Rogers, C. R. (1961). *On becoming a person.* Boston: Houghton Mifflin.

Rosen, J. C., & Wiens, A. N. (1979). Changes in medical problems and use of medical services following psychological intervention. *American Psychologist, 34,* 420-431.

Rosenbaum, R. (1990). Strategic psychotherapy. In *Handbook of the brief psychotherapies,* R. A. Wells & V. J. Giannetti (Eds.), (pp. 351-404). New York: Plenum.

Rosenstein, M. J., & Milazzo-Sayre, L. J. (1981). *Characteristics of admissions to selected mental health facilities 1975.* (DHHS Publication No. ADM 831005). Washington, DC: U. S. Government Printing Office.

Shapiro, D. A., & Shapiro, D. (1982). Meta-analysis of comparative therapy outcome studies: A replication and refinement. *Psychological Bulletin, 92,* 581-604.

Shapiro, D. A., Barkham, M., Rees, A., Hardy, G., Reynolds, S., & Startup, M. (1994). Effects of treatment duration and severity of depression on the effectiveness of cognitive behavioral and psychodynamic-interpersonal psychotherapy. *Journal of Consulting and Clinical Psychology, 62,* 522-534.

Shapiro, D. A., Rees, A., Barkham, M., Hardy, G., Reynold, S., & Startup, M. (1995). Effects of treatment duration and severity of depression on the maintenance of gains after cognitive-behavioral and psychodynamic-interpersonal psychotherapy. *Journal of Consulting and Clinical Psychology, 63,* 378-387.

Shneidman, E. S. (1985). *Definition of suicide.* New York: Wiley.
Sifneos, P. E. (1972). *Short-term psychotherapy and emotional crisis.* Cambridge, MA: Harvard University Press.
Sifneos, P. E. (1987). *Short-term dynamic psychotherapy: Evaluation and technique* (2nd ed.). New York: Plenum.
Silverman, W. H., & Beech, R. P. (1979). Are dropouts, dropouts? *Journal of Community Psychology, 7,* 236-242.
Slaikeu, K. A. (1984). *Crisis intervention.* Boston: Allyn and Bacon.
Sledge, W. H., Moras, K., Hartley, D., & Levine, M. (1990). Effects of time-limited psychotherapy on patient dropout rates. *American Journal of Psychiatry, 147,* 1341-1348.
Sloane, R. B., Staples, F. F., Cristol, A. H., Yorston, N. J., & Whipple, K. (1975). Short-term analytically oriented psychotherapy versus behavior therapy. *American Journal of Psychiatry, 132,* 373-377.
Smith, M. L., Glass, G. V., & Miller, T. I. (1980). *The benefits of psychotherapy.* Baltimore: The Johns Hopkins University Press.
Stiles, W. B., & Shapiro, D. A. (1994). Disabuse of the drug metaphor: Psychotherapy process-outcome correlations. *Journal of Consulting and Clinical Psychology, 62,* 942-948.
Stone, J. L., & Crowthers, V. (1972). Innovations in program and funding of mental health services for blue-collar families. *American Journal of Psychiatry, 24,* 1219-1226.
Straker, M. (1968). Brief psychotherapy in an outpatient clinic: Evolution and evaluation. *American Journal of Psychiatry, 24,* 1219-1226.
Stricker, G., & Gold, J. R. (1993). *Comprehensive handbook of psychotherapy integration.* New York: Plenum Press.
Talmon, M. (1990). *Single-session therapy.* New York: Jossey-Bass.
Taube, C. A., Burns, B. J., & Kessler, L. (1984). Patients of psychiatrists and psychologists in office-based practice: 1980. *American Psychologist, 39,* 1435-1437.
Watzlawick, P., Weakland, H., & Fisch, R. (1974). *Change: Principles of problem formation and problem resolution.* New York: W. W. Norton.
Weinberger, J. (1993). Common factors in psychotherapy. In *Comprehensive Handbook of Psychotherapy Integration,* G. Stricker & J. R. Gold (Eds.), (pp. 43-56). New York: Plenum.
Weiner, J. P. (1994). Forecasting the effects of health reform on U. S. physician workforce requirement: Evidence from HMO staffing patterns. *Journal of the American Medical Association, 272,* 222-230.
Weisz, J. R., & Weiss, B. (1989). Assessing the effects of clinic-based psythotherapy with children and adolescents. *Journal of Consulting and clinical Psychology, 57,* 741-746.
Wells, R. A., & Giannetti, V. J. (Eds.). (1990). *Handbook of brief psychotherapies.* New York: Plenum.
Wierzbicki, M. (1993). *Issues in clinical psychology: Subjective versus objective approaches.* Boston: Allyn & Bacon.

Wierzbicki, M., & Pekarik, G. (1993). A meta-analysis of psychotherapy dropout. *Professional Psychology: Research and Practice, 24,* 190-195.

Wilson, G. T. (1981). Behavior therapy as a short-term therapeutic approach. In *Forms of brief therapy,* S. H. Budman (Ed.), (pp. 131-166). New York: Guilford.

Wolberg, L. R. (1980). *Handbook of short-term psychotherapy.* New York: Thieme-Stratton.

Worden, J. W. (1982). *Grief counseling and grief therapy: A handbook for the mental health practitioner.* New York: Springer.

Wright, R. H. (1992). Toward a political resolution to psychology's dilemmas: Managing managed care. *Independent Practitioner, 12 (3),* 111-113.

Yates, B. T. (1994). Toward the incorporation of costs, cost-effectiveness analysis, and cost-benefit analyses into clinical research. *Journal of Consulting and Clinical Psychology, 62,* 729-736.

Zeig, J. K., & Gilligan, S. G. (1990). *Brief therapy.* New York: Brunner/Mazel.

Index

Abbreviating strategies. *See* Common abbreviating strategies
Abbreviation model, 37-38,42-44
Accountability, 153
Advantages of doing brief therapy, 1-2,149-151
Advocacy for clients, 116
Alcohol abuse, assessment and treatment, 24-25,31,51
Anxiety, treatment of, 126-139
Assessment
  abbreviation of, 49-51,56
  behavioral, 53-57
  Budman and Gurman model, 51-53,56-57
  case example, 72-82,98-99
  components of brief, 49
  of focal issue, case example, 98-99
  importance of brief, 40
  potential risks, 43,50-51
  prerequisite skills, 50-51
  vs. treatment, 113
  with vaguely described problems, 54-55
Attitudes toward brief therapy, xi-xii, 10,27-28,44-45,116
Autonomic arousal, treatment of, 127

"Band-Aid" criticism of brief therapy, 18-19,148
Baldwin, B. A., 5,148
Behavior change, 53-57,112
Behavioral assessment, 53-57
Behavioral dysfunction, 64
Bergin, A. E., 105,112

Bloom, B.L., 5,29,49-50
Brief therapy. *See also* specific brief therapy topics
  anthologies, 48
  history of, 3-8
  impromptu, 128
  theoretical foundation, 5-8
  training, x,154,171-173
  variety of approaches, 37
Budman, S. H., ix,5,20,51-53, 106-108,143,177
Budman and Gurman treatment model, 51-53,56-57
Burnout, 152
Butcher, J. N., 25

Caplan, G., 4-5
Case conceptualization, 47-49,76-79
Case examples of brief therapy, 73-78,95-103,124-139, 159-170
  session-by-session summaries, 133-139,160-169
Child therapy, 23
Client
  advocacy, 116
  autonomy in treatment selection, 32
  characteristics relevant to brief therapy, 29-31
  feeling expression, 110-111
  satisfaction, 156-157
  treatment expectations, and preferences, 11-14,59-60, 62,67,83
Cognitive-behavioral therapy, 5-6, 53-57,106-107,111-112,120
  in case examples, 129,131-132, 139,163-169

187

Cognitive mastery, 109-111
Common abbreviating strategies, xi, 8-10,37,42-44
Common factors in therapy (interventions), 105,107-108. See also Common therapeutic elements; Psychotherapy integration
Common therapeutic elements, xii, 69,105-108
Community mental health centers, 6-7
  treatment duration in, 14
Community resources, use in brief therapy, 116,117
Components of brief therapy. See Common abbreviating strategies
Co-payment, impact of, 151
Cost containment policies, 1,8
Cost effectiveness assessment, 70, 90,153
Cost of therapy, 1,17-18,45
Crisis intervention, 4-5,7,64,102, 106,108
  case examples, 126-128,161-162
Cummings, N. A., 22,154
"Cure," 150

Death, anticipation of,
  and depression, 159-169
Depathologizing, 110
Depression, treatment of, 30-31,110, 156-159
Determinants of therapy efficiency. See Common abbreviating strategies
Distrust of client goals, 43
Dose-effect research, 21,34-35
"Drgs," 30
Dropout
  causes, 13,17-18
  effect of brief therapy on, 2,18
  outcome and, 14,16,23-24
  problems associated with, 17,18

Dropout *(continued)*
  rates, 16
  satisfaction and, 17
Duration of treatment
  actual, 1
  client expectations, 11-12
  client preferences, 12,85
  determinants of, 2
  diagnosis and, 14-15
  negotiation between therapist and client, 85,88-93,100
  and outcome, 18-25,141-142
  prediction of, by therapist, 90,100
  private practice, 14-15
  public clinics, 14
  therapist expectations, 12
  therapist preferences, 13
  variability in brief therapy, xii, 38-39

Early interventions. See First session
Eclecticism, xii,41-42,66,105
Edwards, G., 20,22
Egan, G., 86-87,197
Emotional dysfunction, 64
Empirically validated therapies, 41-42,91
Erikson, E., 7,52
Ethical issues, 1,33-34,92,149
Exercise, as treatment, 135
Existential crisis, treatment
  of in case examples, 163-165

Family therapy, 7,164,168
Feelings, exploration of, 110-111
  in case example, 128-129
First session, 113-114,122,141-143
  outline of tasks, 144-145
Focus, 39,51,59-60
  assessment of, 98-99
  case example, 72-82
  characteristics of, 63
  client preferences, 62,67,78
  flexibility in selection, 80

Focus *(continued)*
  narrowing, 65-66
  obstacles to maintenance of, 62, 67-69,76-77
  practice exercise, 68-70
  priorities, 51,52,63-67,77
  rationale, 59-60
  selection strategies, 61-68
  standard vs. brief therapy, 60-61
  summary, 71-72
  theoretical orientation, 66-67
Frank, J. D., 109
Freud, S., 3

Garfield, S. L., 105,112
Goals
  accomplished after termination, 85
  appropriate, 102
  case example, 95-103,160-161
  change during therapy, 93
  characteristics, 86-87
  consumer-oriented, 83
  contribution to therapeutic relationship, 83-84
  cost-benefit assessment, 89
  and ethics, 92
  implicit vs. explicit, 96
  in long-term therapy, 84
  negotiation strategies, 87-94
  predicting attainment, 92-93
  rationale for modest, 39-40,83
  relationship to treatment duration, 85,88,90
  as termination criteria, 93
  and theoretical orientation, 87-88
  short-term, 116-119
Grief, 110
Group supervision, 171-173
Gurman, A. S., ix,5,20,51-53, 106-108,177

History of brief therapy, 3-8
Homework in brief therapy, 123
Howard, K. I., 20-21,141-142

Impromptu brief therapy, 23-24
Ingredients of brief therapy.
  See Common abbreviating strategies
Inpatient treatment, 24-25
Insomnia, treatment of, 126-127
Insurance reimbursement policies.
  See Co-payment, impact of;
  Service delivery systems
Integrative model for brief therapy, 108-113
Interventions. *See* Treatment

Koss, M. P., 25,29

Length of treatment. *See* Duration of treatment
Life crisis, 4,63,64
Lindemann, E., 4
Long-term therapy, 33-34
  advantages for therapist, 149,152
  conditions that warrant, 34
  outcome for, 19
  selection criteria for, 27-28
  therapist attitude and preference for, 19,148

Managed care, 1,2
Marital problems. *See* Relationship problems
Medical disorders, in depression, 159-162
Medical treatment
  brief therapy impact on, 21-22
  ethics, 32
  noncompliance, 17
Mid-life crisis, 73
Miller, W. R., 22,31
Moral authority in treatment decisions, 32
Myths and misconceptions about brief therapy, 148

"Naming" problems, 109-110
Noncompliance with treatment, 14,17
"Normalizing" problems, 110-111

Obstacles to therapy abbreviation, 147-153
Operational definition of treatment focus, 54
Outcome research for brief and longer therapy, 18-26,29-31
Outcome of therapy
 brief vs. no treatment, 20
 child therapy, 23
 client vs. therapist evaluation, 21
 inpatient, 24
 single session treatment, 22-23
 substance abuse, 22-23
 and treatment duration, 20-21
 and treatment satisfaction, 21
 time-limited vs. time-unlimited, 19-20

Paperwork demands, 153
Performance anxiety, 99
Personality disorders, 65,76
Pleasant activities, in depression, 164-167
Pre-intervention therapist activities, 113
Premature termination. See Dropout; Noncompliance
Pretherapy preparation, 14
Problem-solving therapy, 111-112, 123,129
Procrastination, treatment of, 99
Psychodynamic brief therapy, 7,8, 119-120
Psychotherapy integration, 105-113. See also Common factors in therapy
Psychotherapy subculture, 147

Quality assurance, 153

Rational thinking, 110-111
 in case example, 129
Rationale for brief therapy, importance of training, 154
Reimbursement policies, 151
Relationship problems, treatment of, 73-82
Research recommendations, 34-35
Resistance to brief therapy, 27-28, 147-149
Retraining traditional therapists, 154
Rogers, C. R., 109

Schools of therapy, ix-x. See also Psychotherapy integration
Second session, 145
Selection criteria for brief and longer therapy, 25,27-36
Service delivery systems
 impact on brief therapy, 151
 ways to affect, 151-153
Sexual arousal problems, treatment of, 167-168
Shapiro, D. A., 30-31
Simultaneous use of interventions, 122-123
Single session therapy, 22-24, 119,173
Single, circumscribed problems, 63-64
Slaikeu, K. A., 106-108
Social class, 6,30
Social disorganization, as selection factor in brief treatment, 31
Strategic therapies, 7,120-121
Stressors, 40
Substance abuse, 24-25,31,51
Suicide assessment, 51

Taube, C. A. 14-15
Termination criteria, 93

Theoretical orientation, ix-xi, 9,37-38,47-49,63,66,84, 87,105
Therapeutic elements of brief therapy, 113. *See also* Psychotherapy integration
Therapeutic relationship, 83,106, 109,162
Therapist
  activity, 41
  characteristics suited to brief therapy, 150
  flexibility, 128
  influence on treatment selection, 32-33
  misperception of treatment duration, 15
  motivation to use brief therapy, xii
  rejection by clients, 149
  role contusion, 1-2
  skill, 44,114-116
  treatment expectations, 12-14
Therapy subculture, 19,44
Time limitations and flexibility, 38-39
Training
  components of successful programs, 155

Training *(continued)*
  effects, 154-157
  impact on client satisfaction, 156
  impact on use of brief therapy, 156
  issues, 154-158,171,173
  research, 154-158
Transtheoretical model of therapy, 105,158
Trauma, 111
Treatment
  abbreviation. *See* Common abbreviating strategies
  access, 6
  vs. assessment, 124-126
  client expectations, 11-14,59
  complexity, and simplification of, 118
  duration. *See* Duration of therapy
  outline, session-by-session, 144-145
  planning, 103,131,144-145
  techniques suitable to brief therapy, 105,115-124

Violence potential, assessment of, 51

Wolberg, L. R., ix,8,122